Seventh Edition

Family Financial Management

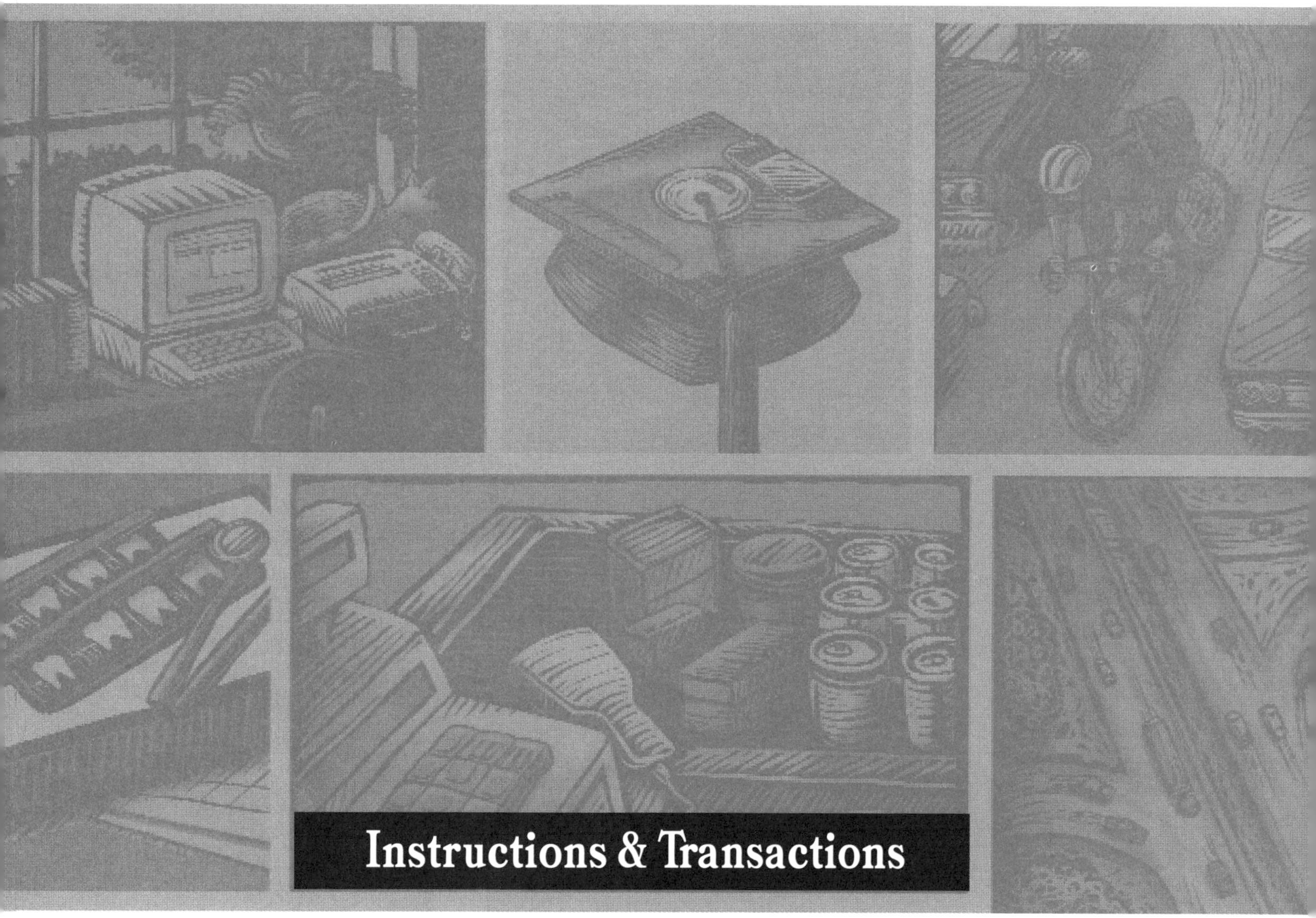

Instructions & Transactions

Australia • Brazil • Japan • Korea • Mexico • Singapore • Spain • United Kingdom • United States

SOUTH-WESTERN CENGAGE Learning

Family Financial Management, Seventh Edition

VP/Editorial Director:
Jack W. Calhoun

VP/Executive Editor:
Dave Shaut

Senior Publisher:
Karen Schmohe

Executive Editor:
Eve Lewis

Project Manager:
Carol Sturzenberger

Director Educational Marketing:
Carol Volz

Senior Marketing Manager:
Nancy A. Long

Marketing Coordinator:
Angela A. Russo

Production Manager:
Patricia Matthews Boies

Production Editor:
Elizabeth Lowry

Cover and Internal Designer:
Bethany Casey

Writer:
Cinci Stowell, Stowell Editorial Services

Reviewer:
Betty Allgood
Teacher, Business Department
Dan River High School
Ringgold, VA

Production House:
electro-publishing

Manufacturing Coordinator:
Kevin L. Kluck

Cover and Internal Images:
©Chet Phillips/Getty Images

Printer:
Globus Printing, Minster, OH

COPYRIGHT © 2005
South-Western, a part of Cengage Learning. Cengage Learning, the Cengage Learning logo, and South-Western are trademarks used herein under license.

Printed in the United States of America
3 4 5 6 7 12 11 10 09

ISBN-13: 978-0-538-43804-9
ISBN-10: 0-538-43804-5

ALL RIGHTS RESERVED. No part of this work covered by the copyright hereon may be reproduced or used in any form or by any means—graphic, electronic, or mechanical, including photocopying, recording, taping, Web distribution or information storage and retrieval systems—without the written permission of the publisher.

For permission to use material from this text or product, submit a request online at www.cengage.com/permissions.

For more information contact South-Western Cengage Learning, 5191 Natorp Boulevard, Mason, Ohio, 45040.
Or you can visit our Internet site at: school.cengage.com

Contents

Introduction ... iii

Phase 1
On Your Own ... 1

Phase 2
Raising a Family ... 18

Phase 3
Investing in the Future ... 36

Forms and Documents ... 51

Glossary ... 154

Introduction

"Wow, your parents' house is so much nicer than ours," said Jamal as he sat relaxing on the deck. "Their backyard is much larger than mine."

"Yeah, my sister and I loved growing up here," replied Ryan. "We used to dream up all kinds of games to play in this yard."

"That's what Keisha and I want to give our children someday," said Jamal. "We're thinking that we should start saving for a down payment on a bigger house."

"Saving!" Ryan laughed. "That's tough. I can't even save enough money for a DVD player."

Ryan was visiting his parents, Sandy and Chad Davis. His parents were enjoying the last days of summer by hosting a backyard cookout. They had invited Ryan, their daughter Tori and granddaughter Carmen, and several friends and neighbors, including Jamal and Keisha Booker, who lived around the corner. Chad grilled hamburgers, while Tori, Carmen, and some of the other guests played games in the yard.

"Ryan," said his mother, Sandy, "I thought you were planning to buy a DVD system months ago."

"I was," he replied, "but I just never seem to have enough money. It's like I'm not in control of my spending."

"I remember being the same way when I was your age," said Jamal. "I had enough money for rent and stuff, but I could never scrape together enough money for big purchases. Keisha helped me start paying attention to our money."

As Jamal said this, Keisha joined them on the deck. "Yes, Jamal," she chuckled. "I seem to recall that you had a little trouble living within our budget at first."

Jamal laughed and hugged his wife. "You're right, I did. But I got used to it. Come to think of it, Ryan, have you ever tried to make a budget for yourself?"

"No, not really. I'm not even sure what a budget is."

"It's simple," said Jamal. "A budget is a plan for your money—so you'll know where it's going. If you want, we can get together sometime and I'll show you how to make a budget."

"Thanks, Jamal," said Ryan with a smile. "I think I could use the help."

The fact is, every person at every age has to deal with money. We all have to plan how we're going to earn money and what we're going to do with it when we get it. It doesn't matter how much money you earn, or how old you are, or if you're single or married, you still have to think about your money, or your *finances*. And everyone has to form a plan, or *budget*, for how to spend and save money. A budget will help you plan for necessary expenses and use the rest of your income to buy or save for the things you want most.

In this simulation, you're going to take a look at the financial circumstances of several people: a young single person, a single mother with one child, and a married couple in their thirties who don't have any children. In each of the three situations, you'll go through one month's worth of money-related events to see how these people keep track of their money and how they make decisions about their finances. Although their lives, incomes, and goals are very different, you'll discover how they all share a need to plan for their money.

We'll begin each phase by introducing you to the characters in more detail. You will see how they figure out their *net worth* (how much they own minus how much they owe) and create their budgets. Then, day by day, we'll show you what happens to their finances—when paychecks come in and when they pay bills and make purchases. You are responsible for helping the characters keep track of all this money coming in and going out. And every once in awhile, we'll ask you a few questions to help you think about why these events and decisions are so important.

To help you keep track of all the financial activities, we've provided several important items in this simulation:

- A *Financial Record Book* where you will write down all the money received and spent over the course of the month. (Some students may receive a computer disk for this purpose.)
- A checkbook to practice writing checks. The checkbook includes a *checkbook register* that you will use to record deposits, written checks, and electronic transactions.
- A *Forms and Documents* section at the back of this instruction book. This section contains all the forms, receipts, and other documents related to the characters.
- A file folder with tabbed dividers for organizing all of the used forms and documents.

Locate each of these items. Tell your teacher if any item is missing. Place the tabbed dividers in alphabetical order in the simulation file folder: Checks Written, Deposits, Forms, Receipts. As you complete the transactions, file the documents behind the proper tab in the file folder. When you finish work each day, store this instruction book in the file folder, in front of the four tabs.

Are you ready to learn more about money, finances, and budgeting? Let's begin with Ryan, a young, single guy who's just learning about financial planning.

On Your Own

Phase 1

RYAN T. DAVIS

Ryan T. Davis is 24 years old. He lives alone in his own apartment at 223 Creek Road, Apt. 5, Maplewood, OH 44920. It's a small, one-bedroom apartment in an older building that doesn't have any extras like a pool or gym. Ryan pays $450.00 a month to live there. The rent includes the cost of some *utilities*, or essential services. The utilities included in his rent are water and garbage pickup, but not gas and electricity. He pays for gas and electricity and for phone service separately. His phone number is (419) 555-2010. His social security number is 333-22-8888. Ryan also owns a used car that his parents bought for him a few years ago. Every month, he gives them a check for $100.00 to pay them back.

Three years ago, Ryan graduated from the local community college with an associate's degree in business management. Now he works full time as the assistant manager of the Crossroads Inn, a family-style restaurant. He receives one paycheck on the first of every month. Ryan's boss is training him to become the manager in a few months. Someday, Ryan would like to own his own restaurant, maybe a fast-food *franchise*. When Ryan is not working, he likes to hang out with his friends, usually playing basketball or watching sports on TV.

Ryan earns $25,000 a year, and he tries to be careful with his money. He doesn't have any credit cards, so he writes checks to pay for bills and larger expenses. Lately, he hasn't been happy with the way he's been spending and the fact that he can't seem to save any money for expensive things, like a DVD system or furniture. Maybe his friend Jamal can help him take control of his money by showing him how to plan a budget.

Performance Outcomes

In the first phase of this simulation, you will learn to:

1. Determine a single person's net worth, a summary of how much the person owns and how much he or she owes.
2. Plan a realistic budget for a single person, based on his or her income.
3. Record a person's daily financial activities in a record book or in a computer file.
4. Organize the receipts, forms, and other paperwork involved in financial activities.
5. Maintain a checking account, including making deposits, writing checks, and balancing a checkbook register.
6. Use an automated teller machine (ATM) and a debit card.
7. Make smart purchasing decisions that fit within a person's budget.
8. Evaluate a person's financial activities at the end of each month to make sure he or she is accurately keeping track of money and living within the budget.

Special Topic: How a Budget Puts You in Control

Knowing where your money comes from and, more important, where it's going is the heart of smart financial management. Together, a plan for income, spending, and saving is called a *budget,* and a budget is what puts you in control of your money. What do you think it means to plan for your money?

Let's pretend you receive a paycheck for $70, and you won't receive another one for the next two weeks. You cash the check and put the cash in your wallet. Then you go out with your friends and buy pizza for everyone, or you go to the store and buy those new shoes you've been wanting. It won't take long to spend all the money you have, will it? So how do you pay for things you need and want until you receive more money? You don't. And what if you want to buy something that costs more than all the money you have at one time? You can't. When you're living like this, you're not in control of your money.

Now, let's imagine doing things a little differently. Before you cash that $70 paycheck, think about what expenses you have coming up. You know you spend about $6 in bus fare each week, or $12 per paycheck. Also, you've set a goal to put $25 from every paycheck in your savings account so that someday you can buy a car of your own. Knowing that you'll need $37 for these two expenses in the next two weeks, you decide to set that money aside, which gives you the freedom to spend the other $33 on movie tickets, CDs, or anything else you want. You can relax because you used a budget to plan for expenses.

Living within a budget allows you to meet your yearly, monthly, and daily expenses and to save for the future. It also means you won't have to borrow money from someone else. Living within a budget puts you in control.

FIGURING OUT RYAN'S NET WORTH

Shortly after the backyard cookout, Ryan and Jamal sat down to take a look at Ryan's finances. Jamal explained that Ryan should first figure out his net worth, so he would know how much money he really has.

Gathering Information

Ryan made a list of his *assets*, or the cash and other items he owns that are worth money:

- $740.12 in a checking account
- $69.65 in a savings account
- A savings bond worth $200.00 given to him by his grandmother
- Current value of his used car, $3,700.00
- Value of his personal items, $1,200.00
- $30.00 in cash

Then he made a list of his *liabilities*, or the money he owes:

- $1,400.00 to his parents for his car
- October rent, $450.00
- Tri-County Gas & Electric bill, $42.53
- Maplewood Telephone Company bill, $35.95

Filling Out the Form

Jamal and Ryan used a form to figure out Ryan's net worth. You can find the answer for yourself. Remove Form 1, page 51 of the *Forms and Documents* section of this instruction book, or access NETWORTH on your data disk. Complete the form using the amounts shown above.

1. Write *Ryan T. Davis* on the blank line at the top.
2. Complete the assets section.
    a. List the amount of each asset in the proper space on the left-hand side of the form.
    b. Add the amounts and write the total amount on the correct line.
3. Complete the liabilities section.
    a. List the amount of each liability on the right-hand side of the form.
    b. Add the amounts and write the total amount on the correct line.
4. Determine Ryan's net worth by subtracting the total liabilities from the total assets, and write the difference on the correct line.
5. Math check: Add the total liabilities and the net worth together. That amount should equal the total assets. If not, go back and check your calculations.
6. File Form 1 behind the *Forms* tab in your file folder, or save your document as RDNWORTH on the disk.

   Notice how Ryan's assets are greater than his liabilities. It's important for the assets amount to be higher, ideally more than double. Otherwise, Ryan would owe more money than he has.

Phase One *On Your Own*

PLANNING RYAN'S BUDGET

Next, Ryan and Jamal planned a budget based on Ryan's income, the money he earns from his job. They started by using a recent *paycheck stub* (Illustration 1) to see how much money he takes home each month. Follow along by removing Form 2 from page 51 in the *Forms and Documents* section, or by accessing BUDGET on your data disk. Be sure to put Ryan's name in the heading.

Illustration 1: Ryan's Paycheck Stub for August

Crossroads Inn

270 Highland Blvd.
Maplewood, OH 44921

Earnings Statement

Check Issued: 9/1/--
Pay Period: 8/1/-- to 8/31/--
Ryan T. Davis
223 Creek Road, Apt. 5
Maplewood, OH 44920
SSN: 333-22-8888

	This Period	Year-to-Date
Gross Pay	$2,083.33	$16,666.64
Deductions		
Federal Income Tax	227.37	1,818.96
Social Security Tax	137.37	1,098.96
State Income Tax	62.50	500.00
City Income Tax	54.17	433.36
Medicare Tax	39.92	319.36
Health Insurance	35.00	280.00
Net Pay	$1,527.00	$12,216.00

Monthly Income

1. Transfer the amount of monthly Gross Pay shown on the paycheck stub to the line marked *Gross Pay* in the upper section of the budget worksheet. *Gross pay* is the total earned before taxes and other deductions have been subtracted.
2. Add the amounts for taxes and deductions shown on the paycheck stub, and record the total on the line marked *Taxes/Deductions.*
3. Deduct the amount for Taxes/Deductions from the amount for Gross Pay, and record the final amount on the line marked *Net Pay.* *Net pay* is the amount of money you take home after taxes and other deductions have been removed.
4. Math check: The amount of Net Pay plus all taxes and deductions should equal Gross Pay.

Now that Ryan knows he has $1,527.00 to work with each month, he can start planning how to spend and save it.

Phase One *On Your Own*

Monthly Expenses

Jamal explained to Ryan that he should fill out the expense categories in the lower portion of the worksheet using real information taken from old receipts and bills. Ryan understood that but pointed out that some expenses change each month. Jamal told Ryan that he should *average* his expenses for the categories that vary. To find the average of a category, he should add up all the amounts in the category. Then divide the total by the number of amounts he added. The result is a "typical" amount for that category. For example, Ryan's phone bill varies each month, depending on how many long-distance calls he makes. To find the average amount he spends per month for phone service, he could add up all his monthly phone bills for last year (12 months). Then divide the total by 12 months.

Ryan also pointed out that some expenses are required, like rent, while others are his choice, like eating out. For expenses that are his choice, Jamal advised him to record an amount he would like to spend for each category, being as realistic as he can. If his planned spending turns out to be more than his income, he will have to go back and adjust his budget by reducing the amounts he can spend in these categories.

Here's how Ryan figured out each category:

1. **Savings/Debt Payoff**. Since this is the category that Ryan wanted to change the most, he put down $120.00 as his goal. Enter $120.00 for Savings Accounts under *Savings/Debt Payoff*.

2. **Home**. Ryan knows he spends $450.00 a month on rent. His average gas and electric bill is $45.00, and his average phone bill is $40.00. Enter these amounts on the correct lines under *Home*. Since Ryan doesn't spend money on the other categories shown on the form, you can enter 0 or leave those lines blank.

3. **Food/Sundries**. Ryan estimates he spends an average of $50.00 a week, or a total of $200.00 per month, on food and sundries. *Sundries* are small personal items, such as toothpaste and shampoo, or small items for your home, such as light bulbs, toilet paper, etc. He decided to divide up this total into these categories: $130.00 for food, $45.00 for personal items, and $25.00 for home care items. Enter these amounts on the correct lines.

4. **Personal**. Ryan decided to set aside $90.00 for clothing and shoes, $25.00 for monthly haircuts, and $40.00 for using the coin-operated laundry machines. Enter these amounts on the correct lines.

5. **Transportation**. Ryan gives his parents $100.00 a month to pay off his car. His car insurance is $120.00 a month, and he thinks he spends about $60.00 on gasoline and oil. Ryan isn't sure how much he should set aside for maintenance. He doesn't have to make repairs very often, but Jamal pointed out that when tune-ups and new tires come along, they're expensive. Ryan decided to set aside a sizable amount of $50.00 monthly so that he'd be prepared for big car maintenance expenses. He also decided to set aside $7.00 per month to save up for once-a-year license and registration fees. Enter these amounts on the correct lines.

6. **Entertainment**. Jamal explained that this category includes such expenses as eating out, movie tickets, dates, and sporting events. Ryan decided to set aside $50.00 for restaurant meals and $40.00 for events, but nothing for travel expenses. Enter these amounts on the appropriate lines.

7. **Miscellaneous**. At first, Ryan didn't think he needed any money here, but Jamal pointed out how many birthday and Christmas gifts he buys each year. Ryan decided to set aside $25.00 for gifts, and then added another $15.00 for hobbies. Ryan also remembered that his bank charges a $10.00 fee each month for his checking account. Enter these amounts on the correct lines.

8. **Health Care**. Ryan is very fortunate to have health insurance that helps him pay his medical costs, which could become very expensive if he should get sick or need an operation. His employer pays part of the insurance *premium*, the regular payment required for an insurance policy. The rest of the premium is deducted from Ryan's paycheck. Ryan's health insurance plan is called a *health maintenance organization (HMO)*. Under this plan, the insurance company pays for most of his medical and dental expenses. When he needs to go to the doctor, he pays only a small fee, called a *copayment*, of $15.00. His copayment for prescription medicine is $10.00. In his budget, Ryan decided to set aside $15.00 for each of these two categories in case he needs medical care sometime. Enter these figures on the correct lines.

9. Math check: When he finished filling out his individual expenses, Ryan totaled the amounts in each category and in each column, finally arriving at a grand total for all categories. He found he was planning to spend $1,517.00 each month. Total Ryan's expenses for yourself to see if the answers on your form match his.

10. According to Ryan's paycheck stub, he brings home $1,527.00, or $10.00 more than his planned spending. He can choose to spend or save this money. Since saving is important to Ryan, he decided to increase his savings goal from $120.00 to $130.00. Enter this change on the budget worksheet and adjust your totals. Now his total planned spending and saving should equal his monthly net pay of $1,527.00.

11. File Ryan's final budget worksheet behind the *Forms* tab in your file folder, or save your document as RDBUDGET.

Now Ryan has a plan for spending and saving. Let's go through one month of his financial activities to see how well he stays within this budget.

THINK IT THROUGH

1. Do you think that this set of budget categories is the only way you could organize your budget? If not, what are some other categories you could use or create?
2. What budget categories would these items fall into: postage stamps? a book about personal finances? a bottle of pain reliever?

RECORDING RYAN'S TRANSACTIONS

Jamal explained that the key to keeping track of money is to record every transaction in one master record. A *transaction* is any event that involves money coming in or going out. To see how this works, you're going to record all of Ryan's transactions in a *Financial Record Book* or in a similar computer file. This ongoing activity will show you exactly how much money he has on any given day, and it will also help you see if Ryan stays within his budget.

Look at the *Financial Record Book*, or call up the file called FINREC on your data disk. Read the headings across the top. For every transaction, record the date and a brief description of the transaction. Use a pencil if you are not working with a computer file. Record all deposits in the *Deposit* column, but record payments under the proper budget categories. For example, if Ryan buys some new clothes, record the cost of the clothes under the *Personal* category.

The last step in recording each transaction is to add the deposit or subtract the payment from the amount in the *Balance* column. The result is the current balance—the total amount in the account after the transaction. Record the current balance in the *Balance* column on the same line as the transaction. Illustration 2 shows how parts of Ryan's filled-out financial record should look.

As you work through each day in Ryan's month, you'll work with receipts and other papers. After each work session of recording transactions, file the receipts and papers behind the proper tabs in your file folder. If you're using the data disk, save this file as RDOCTOBR. Then, check off the box next to each day you've completed so you'll know which transactions you've recorded.

Illustration 2: A Filled-Out Financial Record

	Date	Description	Deposit	Savings/Debt Payoff	Home	Food/Sundries	Personal	Transportation	Entertainment	Miscellaneous	Health Care	Balance
1	10/1	Opening Balance										770 12
2	10/2	Wages	1,527 00									2,297 12
3	10/3	Rent (Valley Apartments)			450 00							1,847 12
4												
5												
6												
7												

OCTOBER TRANSACTIONS

October 1

☐ **1.** Open the first page of the *Financial Record Book* or the computer file. In the *Balance* column of the first line, enter Ryan's total amount of "spendable money." It is $770.12 ($740.12 in checking + $30.00 in cash). Record the date as 10/1 and the description as Opening Balance. Since this amount is not a deposit, but merely the starting point of Ryan's new system, record the amount only in the *Balance* column. Your form should look like Illustration 2, line 1.

The amount of money Ryan has in his checking account should also be recorded in his checkbook register. Find the checkbook included in this simulation package. On the first page of the checkbook register, enter $740.12 in the upper-right corner labeled *Balance Fwd* to indicate that this amount is Ryan's current balance, or total amount in the account at this time. Your checkbook register should show the $740.12 recorded as in Illustration 3 below.

Illustration 3: A Filled-Out Checkbook Register

	CHECK NUMBER	DATE	DESCRIPTION OF TRANSACTION	PAYMENT/ DEBIT (–)	FEE (–)	✓	DEPOSIT/ CREDIT (+)	BALANCE FWD $ 740 12
1	DEP	10/2	Wages	$			$1,527 00	1,527 00
2								2,267 12
3	101	10/3	Valley Apartments	450 00				450 00
4								1,817 12

Phase One   On Your Own   7

Financial Record Categories

Savings/Debt Payoff
Savings Accounts
Investments
Loan Payments

Home
Rent/Mortgage Payment
Property Taxes
Utilities (gas, electric, water, garbage disposal services)
Phone/Pager Services
Cable/Satellite TV Service
Internet Service
Home Maintenance
Home/Renter's Insurance
Home Furnishings (furniture, dishwasher, sheets, dishes, etc.)
Home Electronics (TV, computer, sound system, etc.)

Food/Sundries
Food (prepared and eaten at home)
Personal Care Items (shampoo, toothpaste, etc.)
Small Home Care Items (light bulbs, dishwashing liquid, etc.)

Personal
Clothes & Shoes
Haircuts/Salon Services
Dry Cleaning/Laundry
Gym Membership
Life Insurance

Transportation
Car Loan Payment
Car Insurance
Gasoline/Oil
Car Maintenance
License/Registration Fees
Bus/Subway Fares

Entertainment
Restaurant Meals
Event Fees/Tickets (movies, sporting events, etc.)
Travel Expenses (hotels, airline tickets, etc.)

Miscellaneous
Child Care Expenses
Gifts
Donations/Charities
Pet/Hobby Expenses
Education Fees
Bank Service Charges

Health Care
Doctor & Dental Fees
Prescription Medicines
Glasses/Contact Lenses

October 2

☐ **2.** Ryan's monthly paycheck is Form 3, page 53 in the *Forms and Documents* section of this instruction book. Deposit this paycheck into his checking account.

   a. Detach the paycheck from the earnings statement (paycheck stub) by cutting or neatly tearing along the dotted lines. Endorse the paycheck by using a pen to sign it with Ryan's signature, as shown in Illustration 4.

   b. Remove a deposit ticket from the back of the checkbook.

   c. Fill out the deposit ticket by entering the date, bank number from the paycheck, amount, and total, as shown in Illustration 5. (Write the last two numbers of the current year instead of the dashes shown in the illustration.) The bank number is the hyphenated number in the upper-right corner of the check. Ryan's checking account number is already on the deposit ticket.

Phase One *On Your Own*

d. File the paycheck stub behind the *Receipts* tab in the file folder. File the endorsed paycheck and deposit ticket behind the *Deposits* tab.

Illustration 4:
A Paycheck Endorsed for Deposit Only

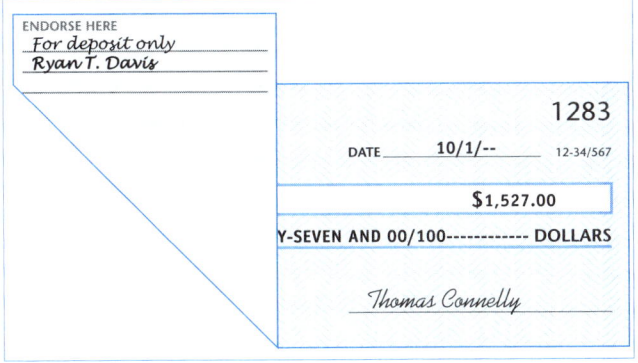

Illustration 5:
A Filled-Out Deposit Ticket for a Check Deposit

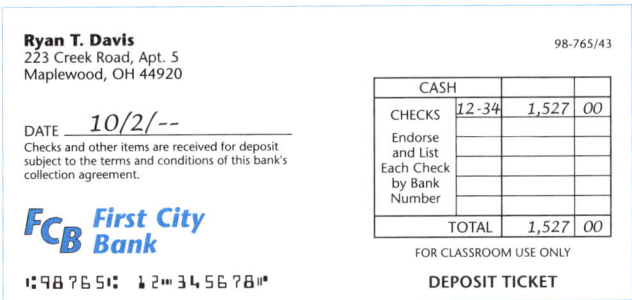

Record Ryan's paycheck deposit in the checkbook register. Write the letters "DEP" under *Check Number* to indicate that this is a deposit, not a written check. Enter the date as 10/2 and the description as Wages. Write the amount, $1,527.00, in the *Deposit* column and in the *Balance* column. (It is copied in the *Balance* column to make adding easier.) Add this amount to the previous balance, and record the total as the current balance in the *Balance* column. Your checkbook register should look like Illustration 3, lines 1 and 2.

Record Ryan's paycheck deposit on line 2 in the *Financial Record Book* or the computer file. Enter the date as 10/2, the description as Wages, and the deposit amount as $1,527.00.

Add this amount to the previous balance, and enter the new total in the *Balance* column. Your form should look like Illustration 2, line 2.

October 3

☐3. Ryan's rent is due anytime between the 1st and the 5th of each month. Remove check 101 from the checkbook to pay Ryan's rent. Use a pen when filling out checks.

a. Fill in the date in the upper-right corner.
b. Make the check payable to Valley Apartments.
c. Next to the $ sign, write the amount, $450.00, using numerals. On the *Dollars* line, write the dollar amount in words and the cents as a fraction of a dollar (100 cents). Use the word "and" only to separate the dollars from the cents. For example, $135.26 would be written as one hundred thirty-five and 26/100.
d. On the line marked *Memo*, write Rent.
e. Sign the check with Ryan's signature.

Your check should look like Illustration 6. File the filled-out check behind the *Checks Written* tab in the file folder.

Illustration 6:
A Filled-Out Check

Record Ryan's rent payment in the checkbook register. Enter the check number as 101 and the date as 10/3. In the *Description* section, write the name of the check's payee. The *payee* is the person or business to whom the check is written. For this transaction, the payee is Valley Apartments. Write the amount, $450.00, in the *Payment* column and in the *Balance* column. (Like deposits, payments are also recorded in the *Balance* column of the checkbook register to make subtracting easier.) Subtract this amount from the previous balance, and enter the current balance in the *Balance* column. This transaction in your checkbook register should look like Illustration 3, lines 3 and 4.

Record Ryan's rent payment on line 3 in the *Financial Record Book* or the computer file. Enter the date as 10/3 and the description as Rent (Valley Apartments). Record the amount, $450.00, under the *Home* column. Subtract this amount from the previous balance, and enter the difference as the current balance in the *Balance* column. This transaction on your form should look like Illustration 2, line 3.

October 5

☐ 4. When Ryan arrives home from work, he decides to check on the two bills he knows are waiting to be paid. The gas and electric bill (Form 4 on page 53 in the *Forms and Documents* section) for $42.53 is due on 10/10, and the phone bill (Form 5, page 55) for $35.95 is due on 10/12. He decides to pay them now so his payments won't be late.

Using the same directions as before, write checks 102 and 103 to pay these bills. However, when you write checks to pay bills, always write the account number on the *Memo* line of the check. You can find the account number printed on the bill. This practice will help your money get to the right place. Your checks should look like those in Illustration 7.

You'll notice that each bill has two sections. Directions on the bill tell you to detach one section and return it with your check. In this simulation, file those sections with the filled-out checks behind the *Checks Written* tab in the file folder. You should keep the other part of each bill as your receipt. File the receipt portion behind the *Receipts* tab in the file folder.

Illustration 7:
Two Filled-Out Checks, Including Billing Account Numbers

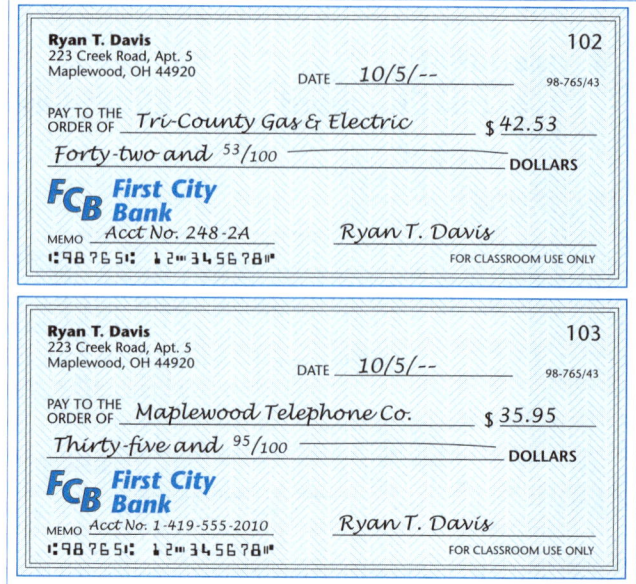

Following the earlier directions, record these two checks in the checkbook register. Be sure to check your math after subtracting the amounts from the previous balance.

Finally, following the directions given before, record these two transactions in the *Financial Record Book* or the computer file. Refer to the list on page 8 whenever you are unsure about which column to use. You can also find this reference list printed at the front of your *Financial Record Book*. Be sure to check your math when you subtract the amounts from the total.

October 6

☐ 5. Ryan stops at the post office to buy stamps. He pays $7.40 in cash. Record the payment in the *Food/Sundries* column in the *Financial Record Book* or the computer file. This is a cash transaction, so do not record it in the checkbook register. File the receipt (Form 6, page 55) in the file folder.

October 8

☐ **6.** Ryan needs to dress nicely for work, so he goes to the mall to buy two new shirts. He likes the expensive designer shirts, but he remembers his budget and decides to buy one less expensive shirt and one medium-priced shirt that's on sale. His total purchase is $79.46.

Write check 104 for $79.46 to Peak Department Stores. Record the transaction in both the checkbook register and the *Financial Record Book* or the computer file. File the receipt (Form 7, page 55) and the check in the correct file folder sections.

7. On his way home, Ryan goes to his favorite small grocery store, Li's Market, for fruit and vegetables because Mrs. Li always has the freshest produce. Ryan pays $10.80 in cash. Record the transaction in the *Financial Record Book* or the computer file, and file the receipt (Form 8 on page 57).

October 9

☐ **8.** Ryan wants to get a debit card from his bank. A *debit card* works like a check. He can use it to pay for purchases at many stores. It also enables him to use an *automated teller machine (ATM)* to make deposits to and withdrawals from his checking account without going inside the bank. So Ryan goes to his bank, First City Bank, to fill out the debit card application. Remove Form 9, page 57, and fill out Ryan's application.

a. Enter Ryan's name, address, phone number, and social security number given in the introduction to Phase 1.

b. Enter the rest of the required information: employer—Crossroads Inn; Phone—(419) 555-6222; occupation—Restaurant Assistant Manager; years employed—2 years, 3 months; Ryan's checking account number—12-345678; mother's maiden name—Alvarez.

c. Sign Ryan's signature and date the application.

When Ryan turns in the application, the teller says he should receive the card in about a week. File the application behind the *Forms* tab in the file folder.

9. While he's at the bank, Ryan asks the teller to withdraw $60 in cash from his checking account. Do not record this transaction in the *Financial Record Book* or the computer file because Ryan is neither depositing nor spending any money at this point. But since this does change his checking account balance, record the transaction in the checkbook register as a withdrawal. Write the letters "WD" under *Check Number* to indicate a withdrawal. Record the date and write Withdrawal in the description section. Record $60.00 in the Payment/Debit column and subtract it from the previous balance. File the withdrawal receipt, Form 10 on page 59, behind the *Receipts* tab in the file folder.

You have completed the first page of the check register. To start a new page, copy the current balance from the bottom of the first page to the *Balance Fwd* column in the upper right corner of the next page.

THINK IT THROUGH

1. Transaction 9 may seem incorrect because it's recorded only in the checkbook register. Can you explain why Ryan should record it this way?
2. Why do you think it's important to keep paycheck stubs, receipts, and forms?

October 11

☐ **10.** Ryan and his friends go to a basketball game at the local college. He pays $10.00 in cash for the ticket, but he doesn't get a receipt. Record the transaction in the *Financial Record Book* or the computer file, and file the ticket stub (Form 11, page 59) as a receipt in the file folder.

October 12

☐ **11.** Ryan goes to his dentist's office for a checkup and cleaning. Because of his HMO insurance through his job, his copayment is $15.00. Write a check to Dr. Sumio Matsumi and record the transaction in both records. File the receipt (Form 12, page 59) and the check in the file folder.

October 13

☐ **12.** A few weeks ago, Ryan's friend Mario asked if Ryan would be willing to sell his old skis. Now that Ryan has thought it over, he's decided to sell the skis because he doesn't go skiing very often and he'd rather have the cash. They agree on a price of $85.00.

Record the $85.00 cash from Mario as a deposit in the *Financial Record Book* or the computer file, because the transaction represents cash coming in. Since he has not yet deposited the money in his checking account, do not record the transaction in the checkbook register.

October 15

☐ **13.** It's time for Ryan to send his monthly car payment to his parents. Write a check for $100.00 to Chad and Sandy Davis. Record the transaction in both record books. File the receipt from Ryan's father (Form 13, page 61) and the check in the file folder.

October 17

☐ **14.** Ryan's debit card (Illustration 8) arrived in today's mail. A letter he received a few days ago assigned his *personal identification number (PIN)*—his "secret code" that allows no one but Ryan to use the card. His PIN is 0101. He decides to use the card to deposit the $85.00 he received from selling his skis. Pretend you're Ryan making the deposit at the ATM. The machine looks similar to Illustration 9.

Illustration 8: A Debit Card

> **FCB   First City Bank**
>
> RYAN T. DAVIS
> 98765 12 345678
>
> DEBIT CARD

a. Remove a deposit ticket from the back of your checkbook and fill it out as before, except enter $85.00 on the line for cash. Your deposit ticket should look like Illustration 10.

b. In Illustration 9, locate the slot for inserting your card and imagine that you are inserting it.

c. When the machine asks for your PIN, key in 0101.

d. When the machine asks what type of transaction you're making, choose Deposit from the menu of choices.

e. When the machine asks what account you're using, choose Checking from the menu of choices.

f. When the machine asks the amount of your transaction, key in 85.00 and press Enter or OK.

Illustration 9:
Parts of an ATM

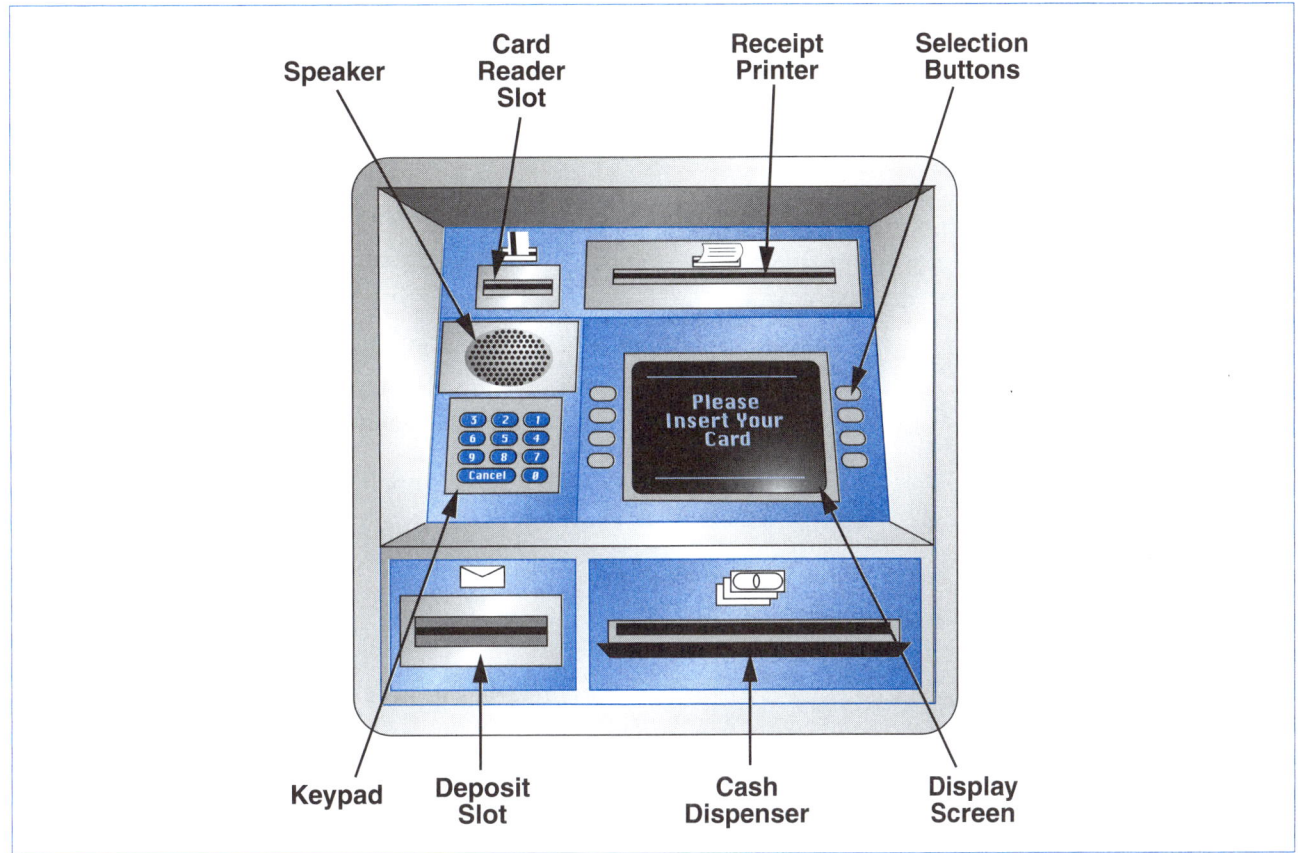

g. When the machine asks if you'd like a receipt, answer Yes.

h. When the machine is ready to receive the envelope with the deposit inside, a slot will open so you can insert the envelope into the machine. (If you were to actually make this deposit using an ATM, you would seal the money and the deposit ticket in an envelope provided at the machine.)

i. The machine prints out a receipt and returns your card.

Different machines use different procedures, but the screen messages will always guide you through the correct steps.

Since you have already recorded this money as a deposit in the *Financial Record Book* or the computer file, you won't record it again. However, since it's now in the checking

Illustration 10:
A Filled-Out Deposit Ticket for a Cash Deposit

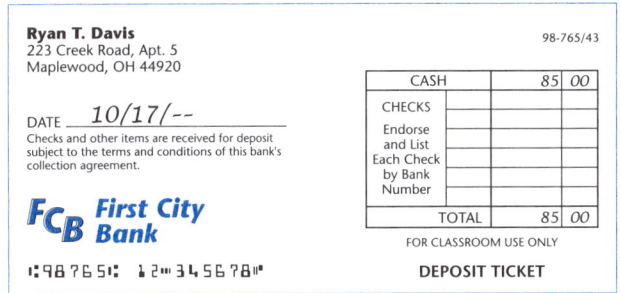

account, and no longer just cash, record the transaction in the checkbook register. In the *Description* column, write ATM Deposit.

Look at the balance shown on the ATM receipt (Form 14, page 61). It does not match the balance in your checkbook register. Why? Ryan gave his parents his car payment two days

Phase One   *On Your Own*   13

ago. They probably cashed or deposited the $100.00 check at their bank. Their bank will then return the check to Ryan's bank so that the amount can be subtracted from his account. Ryan's bank has not yet received the check, so the $100.00 still appears in his balance for now. File the ATM receipt behind the *Deposits* tab in the file folder.

One important note: Whether you're making a deposit or withdrawal, some banks will charge you a *service charge*, or fee, for using their ATMs. If the machine warns you that you will be charged a fee for the service, be sure to record that amount as a payment in your checkbook register.

October 18

☐15. While driving to a friend's house, Ryan fills his car's gas tank. He pays $14.83 in cash. Record the transaction and file the receipt (Form 15, page 61).

October 19

☐16. On his way home from work, Ryan stops at the supermarket for groceries. He uses three coupons (labeled as Form 16 on page 63) for items he was planning to purchase, so his total cost is $33.28. Pretend you're Ryan using the debit card to pay for the groceries.

   a. Slide the card through the machine near the checkout register.
   b. Press the ATM Card button.
   c. Enter the PIN given in Step 14.
   d. When the machine asks "Is 33.28 correct?" press Enter or Okay.

When you make a purchase with a debit card, the amount is immediately withdrawn from your checking account and transferred to the store's account. Record the debit transaction in both the checkbook register and the *Financial Record Book* or the computer file. In the checkbook register, write the letters "DBT" under *Check Number* to indicate a debit transaction. Then file the receipt (Form 17, page 63) in the proper place.

THINK IT THROUGH

1. Ryan would like to buy a pair of basketball shoes for $85. Look at his budget sheet and his financial record. Should he buy the shoes? Why or why not?
2. How might forgetting to record debit card transactions hurt your checking account and your budget?

October 21

☐17. Ryan takes his car in for an oil change for $33.96. However, he accidentally writes the wrong amount of money on the check. To correct his error, he must *void* the check, which is a special process of destroying the check so that no one can cash it. To void a check, write VOID in large letters across the check. Record the check number and date in your checkbook register and write VOID in the description section. Do not record the amount. Instead, draw lines through the Balance space for the voided check. Then start over with a new check.

Write check 107 to Pheng's Garage for the incorrect amount of $23.96. Then void the check. Follow Illustration 11. Write a new check (check 108) for the right amount to correct the error. Record the transaction, and file both checks and the receipt (Form 18, page 65).

October 22

☐18. Ryan's niece is turning two years old next weekend, and he wants to buy her a gift. Before he goes to the store, he checks his budget sheet and learns his spending limit is $25. At the store, he decides to buy a big teddy bear, for a

Illustration 11:
A Voided Check

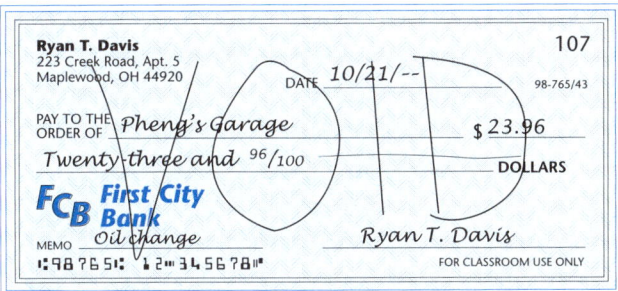

total cost plus tax of $19.49. Write a check to Tracy's Toys, record the transaction, and file the check and receipt (Form 19, page 65).

October 23

☐ **19.** A few days ago, Ryan received his car insurance bill (Form 20, page 67), which is due on 10/30. He decides to pay it today. Write a check to Global Insurance for $120.00. Record the transaction. Then file the receipt and the check with the correct portion of the bill.

October 25

☐ **20.** Ryan's friend Heather has agreed to go on a date with him in a few days, so he gets a haircut. He pays $20.00, plus $3.00 for a tip. Record a cash transaction of $23.00. On the receipt (Form 21, page 67), note the $3.00 tip on the bottom so you won't forget the amount, and file the receipt.

October 28

☐ **21.** Ryan stops at the ATM to get more cash for his date. According to his budget, he can still spend about $80.00 more on socializing this month. He has about $24.00 in his wallet already, so he withdraws $50.00 from the machine. Record the ATM withdrawal in the checkbook register, and file the statement (Form 22, page 67) under *Receipts*.

22. Ryan takes Heather out to dinner and a movie. Their dinner bill is $30.04, plus a $5.00 tip, so he spends $35.04. Movie tickets, plus popcorn and drinks, come to $26.07. Record these cash transactions in the *Financial Record Book* only (you recorded the withdrawal from checking earlier). Note the tip on the bottom of the restaurant receipt and file all the receipts (Form 23, page 69).

October 29

☐ **23.** Ryan reviews his budget and realizes he is within his limits in every category. To transfer his goal amount to his savings account, Ryan writes a check to himself for $130.00. Write the check and record it in the checkbook register. Then use Form 24, page 69, to deposit the money in Ryan's savings account (#12-999999). Illustration 12 shows Ryan's updated savings account balance. Since the amount is no longer "spendable money," record the check as a payment to *Savings* in the *Financial Record Book*. Under *Description*, write Transfer to Savings. File the savings deposit form and check in the file folder.

Now that Ryan has proven to himself that he can live within his budget limits, he wants to make setting aside his savings goal a top priority. In the future, he will transfer money from his checking account to his savings account at the beginning of the month, just after he receives his paycheck.

October 31

☐ **24.** Since it's the last day of the month, Ryan decides to *reconcile* his checkbook and *prove cash* in his financial record. To reconcile his checkbook, Ryan will determine if his bank's checking account statement matches his own checkbook register. To prove cash, he will verify that his *Financial Record Book* records are accurate.

Begin this process by removing Ryan's monthly bank statement for October (Form 25,

Phase One *On Your Own* **15**

Illustration 12: Ryan's Savings Account Statement

First City Bank

RYAN T. DAVIS
223 CREEK ROAD, APT. 5
MAPLEWOOD, OH 44920

Statement For: 9/29/-- to 10/29/--
Beginning Balance: $69.65
Ending Balance: $199.65
Account Number: 12-999999

Regular Savings Account

Date	Description	Amount	Balance
10/29	DEPOSIT	+ 130.00	$199.65

page 71). Find the checkbook register and all of the written checks, deposit tickets, and ATM statements in the file folder. Assume that all of the checks have been processed through the bank, which means they are *cancelled checks*. When you reconcile your checking account in real life, some checks will probably be *outstanding*. These are checks that have not finished their route from the payee's bank to yours. As a result, your bank has not yet *paid* the checks and subtracted the amounts from your account. Most bank statements show the dates the bank paid the checks, not the dates they were written.

a. Compare your records of deposits against the bank statement (Form 25). The statement shows a deposit of $1,527.00 on 10/2 and a deposit of $85.00 on 10/17. You should have two deposit tickets matching these amounts. Now find these entries in your checkbook register. Place a checkmark in the checkmark column next to the entries (see Illustration 13 for an example).

b. Compare your records of written checks, withdrawals, and debit transactions against the bank statement. The statement shows ten cancelled checks, two withdrawals, and one debit transaction. You should have cancelled checks and receipts for all of these transactions. (Your receipt for the debit transaction is the receipt from Holland's Groceries.) Check off each entry as you confirm that the amounts in all three places match exactly.

c. Record any service charges or fees shown on the statement in the *Fee* column in the checkbook register. First City Bank deducts a $10.00 service charge each month from Ryan's

Phase One *On Your Own*

Illustration 13:
A Checkbook Register Showing a Confirmed Entry

CHECK NUMBER	DATE	DESCRIPTION OF TRANSACTION	PAYMENT/ DEBIT (−)	FEE (−)	✓	DEPOSIT/ CREDIT (+)	BALANCE FWD $740 12
DEP	10/2	Wages			✓	$1,527 00	1,527 00
							2,267 12
101	10/3	Valley Apartments	450 00				450 00
							1,817 12

checking account. Enter that amount in the checkbook register in the *Fee* column and code it "SC" for "service charge." Subtract that amount from the balance. Also record the service charge in the *Financial Record Book* or computer file under the *Miscellaneous* category.

d. Math check: Now compare the balance in the checkbook register with the balance on the monthly bank statement. These two amounts should match. If not, go back and check your calculations for each entry in the checkbook register until you find your error.

Return all written checks and other documents to the proper places in the file folder.

25. As you have probably figured out by now, the main difference between the checkbook register and the *Financial Record Book* is that the record book involves cash as well as checks. You can check the accuracy of the balance in the *Financial Record Book* or the computer file by comparing it to the sum of cash Ryan has now plus the balance in his checking account. The ending balance in the record book should equal the ending balance in his checking account plus the cash in his wallet.

Math check: Add Ryan's current cash (which is $12.86) to his checking account balance ($1,172.45). Does this sum equal the balance in the *Financial Record Book* or computer file? If not, go back and check your calculations in the record book to find your error. Keep in mind that the $130.00 deposited into his savings account should not be added back at this stage since it is no longer "spendable" money.

26. As the last step, total each of the payment columns in the *Financial Record Book* or the computer file. Write the totals in the boxes at the bottom of each column. Compare these amounts to Ryan's original budget sheet and note that he's stayed within budget in every category.

THINK IT THROUGH

1. If you were Ryan, how would you feel about your finances and financial decisions for the month of October? How would you feel about your financial decisions since you began working?
2. Are there changes that might occur in Ryan's life that will prompt him to change his budget? What kinds of changes?

Phase One *On Your Own* **17**

Raising a Family

Phase 2

TORI DAVIS-MARTINEZ

Tori Davis-Martinez, Ryan's older sister, is 30 years old. She has a full-time job, and she is raising her two-year-old daughter, Carmen, by herself. She and her husband divorced two years ago.

About eight years ago, Tori earned a bachelor's degree in sociology. In her first few working years, she held several different jobs. But five years ago she began working for a small company called Cabot Services, a property management company. Cabot has grown rapidly since then, so Tori's job duties as human resource manager have grown, too. Although her job can be stressful, Tori enjoys contributing to the careers and lives of other Cabot employees. Tori earns an annual salary of $42,000, and is paid bimonthly (twice a month). Her Social Security number is 111-55-9999.

At home, Tori and Carmen live in a two-bedroom condominium at 4388 Canal Street in Hopewell, Ohio 45313. Their phone number is (937) 555-2262. Tori pays $700.00 a month in rent, which includes water and garbage pickup. She pays for gas and electricity, telephone, and cable Internet and TV services separately. One of Tori's biggest expenses is child care for her daughter, but she knows that providing a safe place for Carmen is worth every penny. Tori and Carmen are fairly comfortable, but Tori suspects she's going to have to buy a new car soon. She doesn't have enough money in savings to pay for the car completely. She'll have to take out a car loan to pay for it. The car she drives now is paid for, so adding a monthly car payment to her expenses will have a major impact on her budget.

Performance Outcomes

In the second phase of this simulation, you will learn to:

1. Prepare a statement of net worth and a budget for a single working parent.
2. Understand the difference between good debt and bad debt.
3. Pay bills and make purchases online.
4. Use a credit card properly.
5. Figure federal income taxes for a single working parent.
6. Apply for a car loan.
7. Use the Internet to research a major purchase.
8. Adjust a budget to allow for a major purchase.
9. Use an interest-bearing checking account.
10. Continue developing solid financial management skills, such as record keeping and decision making.

Special Topic — Credit Showdown: Good Debt vs. Bad Debt

Anytime you buy something and pay for it over time, instead of right away, you are buying on *credit*. Credit is borrowing. It can be a loan from a bank or a line of credit from a credit card company or department store. A *line of credit* is the maximum amount of unpaid debt you can have on that account. For example, if your credit card has a $1,000 line of credit, you may make purchases up to a total of $1,000. As you pay down the debt, however, you may again make purchases on the card, as long as the total does not go over the $1,000 maximum.

Credit allows you to buy products or services now in exchange for a promise to pay in the future. The problem with buying on credit is that you have to pay back more than you borrowed. Your repayment includes interest. *Interest* is additional money you must pay for the privilege of using borrowed money.

Now, you may think that this concept of borrowing and paying back money—even with interest—is a good idea. In some cases, it is. Let's say you want to buy a house that costs $140,000. You're not likely to have that much cash at one time, so you could take out a home loan called a *mortgage*. Perhaps you'll decide to go to an expensive college and qualify for a $60,000 bank loan. With either of these loans, you'll be making payments for quite a few years.

Because a house and a college education generally become more valuable over time, they are considered "good debts."

On the other hand, many people tend to go into debt for purchases that decrease in value. Vacations, clothes, and many other consumer items lose their value over time, and yet people frequently use loans and credit cards to pay for them. Does it make sense to pay the actual purchase price *plus* interest for something that is *losing* its value? Of course not. That's why this type of debt is called "bad debt."

Perhaps the worst thing about bad debt is that it accumulates easily, sometimes to the point that you cannot repay what you owe. So what's the answer? Avoid debt in the first place. Whenever possible, delay buying things until you can pay for them up front. Have no more than one credit card. Multiple lines of credit can tempt you to charge more than you can afford. When you use a credit card, charge no more than you can pay in full when the bill arrives. Then pay off the credit card bill every month. Don't get into the habit of paying only the minimum required. If you do, the high interest rate can keep you in debt for years, and the total interest you pay can be astronomical.

Phase Two *Raising a Family*

FIGURING OUT TORI'S NET WORTH

Do you recall filling out Ryan's net worth worksheet in Phase 1? Now you can do the same for Tori. Remove Form 26 from page 73 of the *Forms and Documents* section of this instruction book, or call up the NETWORT2 file on your data disk. You may need to refer to the directions on page 3 in Phase 1. Use the following information to complete Tori's net worth form:

Assets

- $339.27 in an interest-bearing checking account.
- $4,120.81 in a money market savings account.
- $16,148.37 in a 401(k) retirement savings account.
- $1,000.00 cash value of a life insurance policy.
- Current value of her car, $1,800.00.
- Value of her personal items, $4,300.00.
- $130.00 in cash.

Liabilities

- March rent, $700.00.
- Tri-County Gas & Electric bill, $95.10.
- PBC Telephone Company bill, $44.31.
- Express Cable Service bill (TV & Internet), $86.95.
- S&T Insurance Company bill (auto, renter's, life), $72.00.

Math check: Be sure to check your calculations. Then file Form 26 behind the *Forms* tab of the file folder, or save your document as TMWORTH.

WRITING OUT TORI'S BUDGET

Think about how you filled out Ryan's budget worksheet in Phase 1. Now fill out Tori's worksheet. Remove Form 27 from page 73 of the *Forms and Documents* section of this instruction book, or open BUDGET on the data disk. Tori has been using a budget worksheet to manage her money since she graduated from high school, and she updates it whenever her financial situation changes. Use the information on the next page to complete Tori's current budget.

Math check: Total Tori's monthly expenses. Then, look at her paycheck receipt (stub) (Illustration 14 on page 22). Since Tori receives two paychecks a month (one on the 1st and one on the 15th), her monthly net pay is double what is shown on this paycheck receipt. Does Tori's monthly net pay cover her monthly expenses?

File Tori's budget worksheet behind the *Forms* tab, or save your document as TMBUDGET.

You will now work through a month's worth of financial transactions for Tori. Check the boxes as you complete each day's activities.

Phase Two   *Raising a Family*

Tori's Budget Information

Monthly Income (rounded)
Gross Pay, $3,500.00
Taxes/Deductions, $806.00
Net Pay, $2,694.00

Savings/Debt Payoff
Savings, $50.00

Home
Rent, $700.00
Utilities, $95.00
Phone Service, $44.00
Cable TV Service, $40.00
Cable Internet Service, 47.00
Renter's Insurance, $15.00

Food/Sundries
Food, $260.00
Personal Care Items, $60.00
Home Care Items, $40.00

Personal
Clothes and Shoes, $300.00
Haircuts, etc., $45.00
Dry Cleaning, Laundry, $50.00
Life Insurance Premium, $12.00

Transportation
Car Insurance Premium, $45.00
Gasoline, $80.00

Maintenance, $85.00
License/Registration, $7.00

Entertainment
Restaurant Meals, $90.00
Event Fees/Tickets, $40.00

Miscellaneous
Child Care, $480.00
Gifts, $35.00
Bank Service Charges, $4.00

Health Care
Doctor and Dental Fees, $45.00
Prescription Medicines, $25.00

MARCH TRANSACTIONS

March 1

☐ **1.** On the first page of the *Financial Record Book* for Phase 2, enter Tori's total amount of spendable money ($339.27 in her checking account + $130.00 in cash). Enter the date as 3/1, record the description as Opening balance, and enter the amount in the *Balance* column. Or call up the FINREC document on your data disk, record the opening balance, and save the document as TMMARCH.

Start a new page in the checkbook register and enter Tori's balance of $339.27. Refer to the directions on page 11 in this instruction book, as needed.

March 2

☐ **2.** Tori arranged with her employer to have her bimonthly paychecks deposited automatically into her checking account. This form of payment is called *direct deposit*. On paydays, Tori receives a receipt for the deposit instead of a paycheck. The receipt provides the same information as a paycheck stub. Remove the receipt for Tori's March 1 paycheck (Form 28, page 75), and check that all the information is correct.

a. Check her name, address, and social security number against the information given on page 18 in this instruction book.

b. Tori has chosen to have a portion of each paycheck deposited into a 401(k) account. A *401(k) account* is a special account workers can use to save money, mainly for retirement. You don't have to pay income tax right away on money deposited in a 401(k) account. Your contributions are not taxable until you withdraw the funds, usually at retirement. In most cases, if you withdraw money from your 401(k) account before you reach retirement age, you will have to pay a large financial penalty.

Tori has chosen to contribute 4% of her salary to a 401(k) account, although she plans to increase this percentage as she earns more income. Check to make sure that this deduction is correct. Assume the other tax deductions are correct.

Phase Two   *Raising a Family*

Illustration 14: Tori's Paycheck Receipt

Cabot Services, Inc.

8820 Main Street
Hopewell, OH 45311
(937) 555-3777

Tori Davis-Martinez
4388 Canal Street
Hopewell, OH 45313
SSN: 111-55-9999

Direct Deposit Paycheck Receipt
(This is not a check.)

Date Issued: 3/1/--
Amount Deposited: $1,347.23

Pay	This Period	YTD
Gross Pay	$1,750.00	$7,000.00
Net Pay	$1,347.23	$5,388.92

Deductions	This Period	YTD
401(k)	$ 70.00	$280.00
Federal Tax	$180.60	$722.40
State Tax	$ 31.39	$125.56
Soc. Sec.	$ 59.45	$237.80
Medicare	$ 21.33	$ 85.32
PPO Health Plan	$ 40.00	$160.00

Deposited to:
Hopewell Community Bank
Checking account #: 21-436587

---

c. Check that her bank information is correctly stated as Hopewell Community Bank, checking account #21-436587.

Record the direct deposit in the *Financial Record Book* or computer file and in the checkbook register. File the paycheck receipt behind the *Receipts* tab in the file folder.

March 3

☐ **3.** On her lunch hour, Tori stops to have the oil in her car changed at Easy-Fix Car Care. As the mechanics are working on the car, they discover it needs a new air filter and that oil is leaking from somewhere in the car. Tori feels frustrated because nearly everything about her formerly reliable car is now in need of repair. She thanks the mechanics for noticing the problem and pays for the service with check 672 for $54.78.

Phase Two *Raising a Family*

In this phase and in Phase 3, you will no longer write checks or deposit tickets. However, you will still need to record the checks and deposits in the checkbook register and in the *Financial Record Book* or computer file as directed. Record this transaction in both places. File the receipt (Form 29, page 75) behind the *Receipts* tab in the file folder.

4. Tori's rent isn't due until the 5th, but she likes to pay early to make sure she doesn't forget and get charged a late fee. Record check 673 for $700.00 to Lakeview Properties (the company that owns her condo) in the *Financial Record Book* or computer file and in the checkbook register.

March 4

☐**5.** Tori's bills for her gas and electric, telephone, and cable Internet and TV services are all due within the next week (see Forms 30-32, pages 77-79 of this instruction book). Two months ago, Tori registered at her bank's Web site so that she could pay these bills online. At the site, she followed the step-by-step instructions to enter the personal and checking account information required to set up the online account. She chose a user ID and PIN (personal identification number) that would identify her as the account holder. She wrote down the ID and PIN and put them in a safe place.

Then, following instructions at the site, she entered account numbers and addresses for each bill she wanted to pay online. She had to go through this set-up process only once. Now, each month, she can just select the payee (company) and enter the amount of the bill. The bank will deduct that amount from her checking account and pay the bill.

To pay these bills today, Tori goes to her bank's Internet home page. She follows the same steps to pay each bill, starting with the gas and electric bill. Pretend you are Tori paying bills online. You would use your computer keyboard and mouse to complete these transactions:

a. At the home page, click the link for Online Banking. (Different banks have different names for their links, but the links will be clearly marked and easy to follow.)

b. In the log-in box that appears, enter Tori's user ID: TDM4658 and PIN: 80523, and click Log In. A closed-lock symbol at the bottom of the computer screen tells you that you have entered a secure Web page.

c. Now that Tori has accessed her account, she can view her account balance, review recent transactions, order a new checkbook, or do other transactions. Today, however, she wants to pay bills. Click the Make Payments link.

d. Illustration 15 shows the bill payment Web page for Tori's account. Click the down-arrow next to Payee. You will see the list of payees Tori has set up.

e. Click Tri-County Gas & Electric to select this payee.

f. Enter the payment amount: $95.10.

g. Click OK to transmit the information.

h. The next Web page asks you to review the information you just entered to make sure it is correct. Check to see that you have scheduled the correct payment of $95.10 to Tri-County Gas & Electric.

i. Click Pay to complete the transaction.

j. Repeat the process to pay the phone and cable companies. Be sure to check the payment amounts each time before completing the transaction.

k. When finished, click the Log Out button to end your online session.

Since all three of these payments are made with money from Tori's checking account, record all three transactions in the *Financial Record Book* or computer file and in the checkbook register. In the Check Number column of the checkbook register, write the code ON to indicate a payment made online. In the Description section of the checkbook register and record book, write the name of the payee,

Phase Two   *Raising a Family*

Illustration 15: Tori's Online Bill-Payment Page

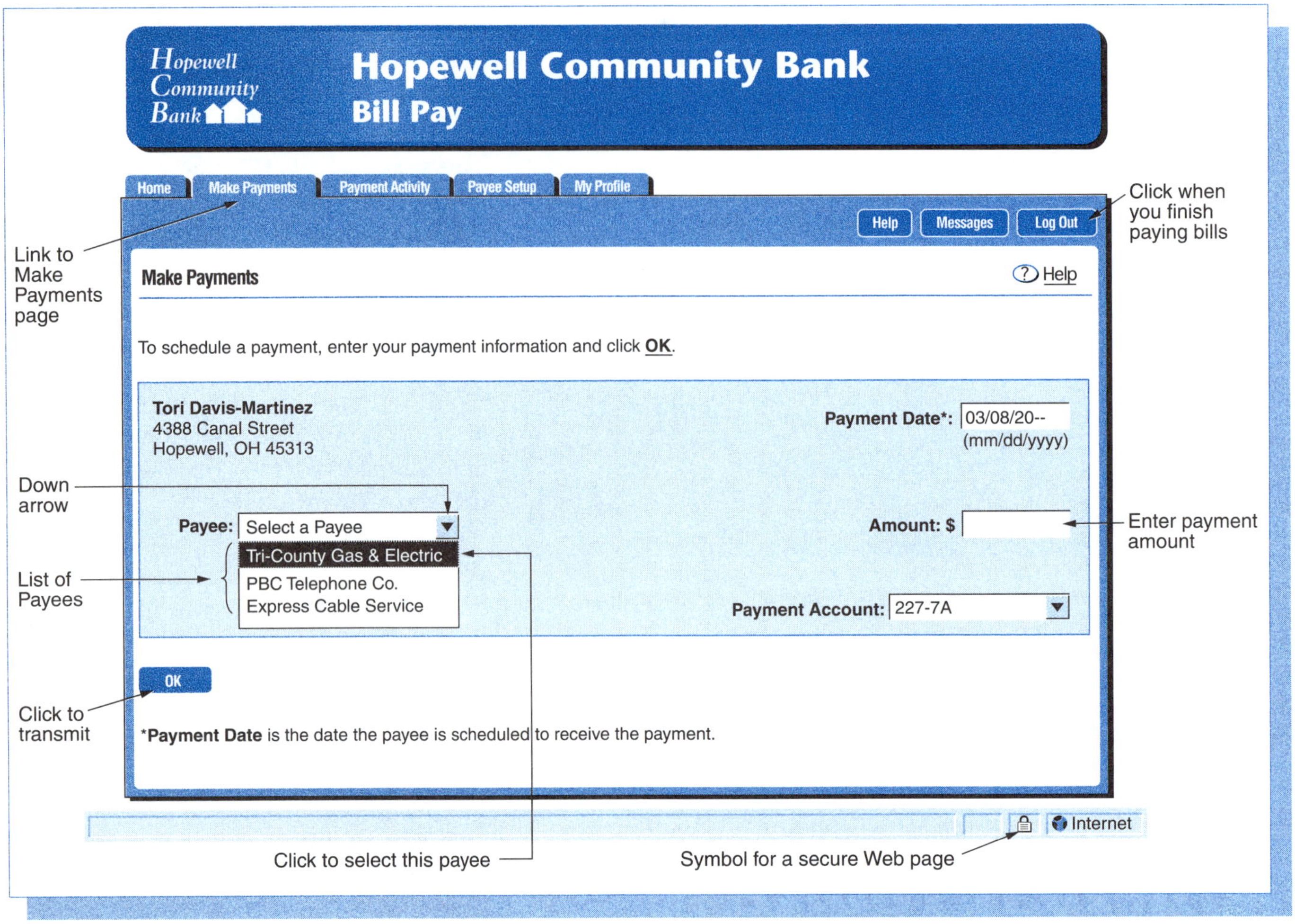

[Screenshot of Hopewell Community Bank Bill Pay page with annotations: Link to Make Payments page; Down arrow; List of Payees; Click to transmit; Click when you finish paying bills; Enter payment amount; Click to select this payee; Symbol for a secure Web page]

just like you would record a check. File the receipt portion of each bill behind the *Receipts* tab of the file folder. Since you don't have to mail checks when you make online payments, you could discard the portion of each bill that would accompany your checks. However, for this practice set, you should file the bill portion behind the *Checks Written* tab.

March 6

☐ **6.** Tori has one all-purpose credit card (Illustration 16). To keep her credit card debt under control, she uses the card only for online purchases and for gasoline. She chose a WorldCard because it does not impose a *finance charge* if she pays off the balance in full each month.

Illustration 16:
Tori's Credit Card

On the way home from work, Tori stops at GasCo to fill her car's gas tank. She uses her credit card to pay $15.24 for the gas. She always saves her receipts so that she can check

24   Phase Two   *Raising a Family*

them against the credit card bill at the end of the month. Record the transaction in the *Financial Record Book* or computer file, and file the receipt (Form 33, page 79). Since this is a credit purchase, Tori will not record the transaction in her checkbook register until she pays the credit card bill later by check.

7. After picking up Carmen from the daycare center, Tori stops at the Hilltop Grocery Store. Her purchases total $79.33. She uses her debit card to pay for the groceries. Debit card transactions are not credit. The payment amount will be immediately deducted from Tori's checking account. Record the transaction in the *Financial Record Book* or computer file and in the checkbook register. File the receipt (Form 34, page 81) in the file folder.

THINK IT THROUGH

1. When is it safe, and when is it not safe, to give your credit card number to another person?
2. How might having more than one credit card encourage you to spend more than you can afford?
3. There's an old saying that "two people can live as cheaply as one." After seeing Tori's budget, do you think this statement is true? Explain your answer.

March 8

☐ **8.** On this Saturday morning, Tori takes her car to her favorite mechanic, Jason Dobbs at Jason's Garage, to check the oil leak. Before leaving the garage, she wisely asks for an *estimate*. This is a written document showing how much a repair or other service is likely to cost. The customer can then decide, before work begins, whether or not to go ahead with the service. Based on the estimate, Tori decides to go ahead and have the car fixed. Mr. Dobbs promises to have the car ready by late this afternoon. File the estimate (Form 35, page 81) behind the *Receipts* tab.

9. Without the car, Tori and Carmen are stuck at home. While Carmen plays with her toys, Tori fills out her income tax forms to figure out how much tax she owes the government on the money she earned last year. Tax forms are due on April 15, and Tori doesn't want to wait until the last minute to fill out the forms. Remove Form 36 from page 83 and follow along as Tori completes this form. Refer to Illustration 17 for information provided by her employer on the W-2 form and by her bank on the 1099 form, as needed. Also, refer to Illustration 18, a page from the income tax directions book, when directed.

a. Fill out Tori's name, address, and social security number from the W-2 form in Illustration 17.

b. In the Filing status section, you must check the one box that best describes Tori's status. Tori is single, but she also provides a home for a dependent child. A *dependent* is a person who relies on someone else for financial support. Because Tory supports a child, she qualifies as the "head of household." Check box 4.

c. The next section helps you figure out the number of exemptions Tori qualifies for. *Exemptions* reduce the amount of income that will be taxed. So, the more exemptions you are allowed to take, the lower your tax. Check the first box for Yourself and write 1 in the box in the right margin. Under 6c, list Carmen Martinez, social security number 634-56-3616, and daughter. Then check the box to indicate that Carmen qualifies for the child tax credit. Write 1 in the second box in the right column because Carmen is also an exemption for Tori. Under 6d, write the total number of exemptions, 2, in the right-hand box.

d. In Illustration 17, locate box 1 on the W-2 form. Write this wage amount on line 7 of the tax form.

Phase Two   *Raising a Family*   **25**

Illustration 17: Tori's W-2 Form and 1099 Form from Last Year

a Control number 22222 Void ☐ For Official Use Only ▶ OMB No. 1545-0008		
b Employer identification number 99-0000099	1 Wages, tips, other compensation $40,320.00	2 Federal income tax withheld $4,233.61
c Employer's name, address, and ZIP code Cabot Services, Inc. 8820 Main Street Hopewell, OH 45311	3 Social security wages $42,000.00	4 Social security tax withheld $1,403.13
	5 Medicare wages and tips $42,000.00	6 Medicare tax withheld $501.06
	7 Social security tips $	8 Allocated tips $
d Employee's social security number 111-55-9999	9 Advance EIC payment $	10 Dependent care benefits $
e Employee's first name and initial: Tori Last name: Davis-Martinez 4388 Canal Street Hopewell, OH 45313	11 Nonqualified plans $	12a See instructions for box 12 E $1,680.00
	13 Statutory employee ☐ Retirement plan ☒ Third-party sick pay ☐	12b $
	14 Other	12c $
		12d $
f Employee's address and ZIP code		
15 State Employer's state ID number OH 23-5555	16 State wages, tips, etc. $40,320.00	17 State income tax $1,272.64	18 Local wages, tips, etc. $40,320.00	19 Local income tax $	20 Locality name Hopewell

Form **W-2** Wage and Tax Statement   **20--**

Form 1099–INT
Statement of Interest Earned

For: Tori Davis-Martinez, 4388 Canal Street, Hopewell, OH 45313
Social Security Number 111-55-9999

Account Number	Account Type	Interest Earned
21–436587	Interest-bearing checking	$47.20
21–909090	Money Market savings	$123.61

e. Line 8 refers to the amount of interest that Tori's bank accounts earned last year. Add the two amounts shown on Form 1099 in Illustration 17, and write the figure, $170.81, on line 8a.

f. Lines 8b through 14b don't apply to Tori. Add lines 7 and 8a together and write the amount on line 15.

g. Lines 16 through 20 also do not apply to Tori. Follow the instructions for line 21. Then transfer the number from line 21 ($40,490.81) to line 22 on the top of page 2.

h. Skip lines 23 a and b, since they don't apply to Tori, and read the directions for line 24. What is Tori's standard

Phase Two *Raising a Family*

deduction? Look back at Tori's filing status (line 4). Since she qualifies as head of household, her deduction is $6,900.00. Write this amount on line 24.

i. Follow the directions on lines 25, 26, and 27, and enter your answers.

j. The answer on line 27 ($27,590.81) is Tori's *taxable income*, the amount of income on which she must pay a tax.

k. To find out how much tax Tori owes, look at Illustration 18. In the left column, locate the range in which Tori's taxable income falls. It is $27,550 to $27,600. Then follow that line across to the right-hand column under *Head of a household*. This amount, $3,636.00, is the amount of tax owed on Tori's taxable income. Write this figure on line 28.

l. *Tax credits* are amounts that taxpayers may subtract from the tax they owe. On the next several lines, you will subtract the tax credits for which Tori qualifies. Tori gets a tax credit because she pays for child care for Carmen. On a separate form not shown here, Tori has determined that her credit amount is $480.00. Write this amount on line 29.

m. Tori doesn't get credit for lines 30 through 32 or 34, but she does qualify for the child tax credit, line 33. On a separate form not shown here, Tori figured this credit to be $600. Write this number on line 33.

n. Follow the directions for lines 35, 36, and 38, and enter your answers on those lines. (Line 37 does not apply to Tori.)

o. Now that her credits have been subtracted, line 38 shows the total tax Tori owes for the year. However, her employer has been taking money out, or *withholding* money, from each paycheck all year long. Cabot Services sends this money to the government as payments on Tori's income taxes. Look at Form W-2 in Illustration 17. The total amount that Cabot withheld for federal income taxes is shown in box 2. Enter the amount,

Illustration 18:
Income Tax Tables from the Income Tax Directions Booklet

If Form 1040A, line 27, is—		And you are—			
At least	But less than	Single	Married filing jointly *	Married filing separately	Head of a household
		Your tax is—			

26,000

26,000	26,050	3,604	3,304	3,925	3,404
26,050	26,100	3,611	3,311	3,938	3,411
26,100	26,150	3,619	3,319	3,952	3,419
26,150	26,200	3,626	3,326	3,965	3,426
26,200	26,250	3,634	3,334	3,979	3,434
26,250	26,300	3,641	3,341	3,992	3,441
26,300	26,350	3,649	3,349	4,006	3,449
26,350	26,400	3,656	3,356	4,019	3,456
26,400	26,450	3,664	3,364	4,033	3,464
26,450	26,500	3,671	3,371	4,046	3,471
26,500	26,550	3,679	3,379	4,060	3,479
26,550	26,600	3,686	3,386	4,073	3,486
26,600	26,650	3,694	3,394	4,087	3,494
26,650	26,700	3,701	3,401	4,100	3,501
26,700	26,750	3,709	3,409	4,114	3,509
26,750	26,800	3,716	3,416	4,127	3,516
26,800	26,850	3,724	3,424	4,141	3,524
26,850	26,900	3,731	3,431	4,154	3,531
26,900	26,950	3,739	3,439	4,168	3,539
26,950	27,000	3,746	3,446	4,181	3,546

27,000

27,000	27,050	3,754	3,454	4,195	3,554
27,050	27,100	3,761	3,461	4,208	3,561
27,100	27,150	3,769	3,469	4,222	3,569
27,150	27,200	3,776	3,476	4,235	3,576
27,200	27,250	3,784	3,484	4,249	3,584
27,250	27,300	3,791	3,491	4,262	3,591
27,300	27,350	3,799	3,499	4,276	3,599
27,350	27,400	3,806	3,506	4,289	3,606
27,400	27,450	3,814	3,514	4,303	3,614
27,450	27,500	3,821	3,521	4,316	3,621
27,500	27,550	3,829	3,529	4,330	3,629
27,550	27,600	3,836	3,536	4,343	3,636
27,600	27,650	3,844	3,544	4,357	3,644
27,650	27,700	3,851	3,551	4,370	3,651
27,700	27,750	3,859	3,559	4,384	3,659
27,750	27,800	3,866	3,566	4,397	3,666
27,800	27,850	3,874	3,574	4,411	3,674
27,850	27,900	3,881	3,581	4,424	3,681
27,900	27,950	3,889	3,589	4,438	3,689
27,950	28,000	3,899	3,596	4,451	3,696

$4,233.61, on lines 39 and 43. (Lines 40-42 do not apply to Tori.)

p. Compare the amount Tori has already paid (line 43) to the tax owed (line 38). Notice that she has paid more than she owes. She will get a *refund* from the government. Find the amount of her refund by subtracting line 38 from line 43. Enter the answer on line 44.

q. Tori decides to have the full amount of her refund deposited directly into her checking account. Fill out lines 45a through d accordingly. Tori's checking account number appears on her Form 1099 in Illustration 17. Tori called her bank to get the routing number for line 45b: 110593822.

r. Sign Tori's signature and add the date and her occupation at the bottom of the form. Fill in her daytime (work) phone number, which is her employer's number: (937) 555-3777.

Tori mails this form, along with copies of her W-2 and 1099, to the Internal Revenue Service. On another day before April 15, Tori will have to follow a similar procedure for determining her state income taxes.

In real life, this form and the information you will need to fill it out will change yearly. Although the process will be similar each year, you'll need to follow the instruction booklet that comes with your tax form each time you figure your taxes.

10. Around 3:00 in the afternoon, Jason Dobbs calls to say the car is ready to be picked up. The total, with tax, comes to $201.40. The actual bill is less than 10% more than the estimate, so it is reasonable. Tori writes a check for the repairs. Record the transaction in the *Financial Record Book* or computer file and in the checkbook register. File the receipt (Form 37, page 85) with the estimate under *Receipts*.

Before she leaves, Tori asks Mr. Dobbs for his opinion about her car. Mr. Dobbs believes the car will need more and more major repairs in the near future. He suggests that perhaps it's time to buy a more reliable car, something Tori expected him to say. She already has been thinking about putting money into payments on a new car, rather than continuing to pay for repairs on the old car.

March 10

☐11. On her lunch hour, Tori goes to the bank. Alex Littlebear, the loan officer at Hopewell Community Bank, gives Tori a car loan application. Remove Form 38 from page 87 and follow along as Tori fills out this application.

a. Next to Branch, write Sherwood.

b. Under Purpose, write Car loan.

c. Under Amount Requested, write $16,000.00, even though Tori probably won't need to borrow that much.

d. Under Terms Requested, write the time needed to pay off the loan, which in this case is five years (or 60 months).

e. Under Applicant Information, find Tori's full name, address, phone number, and social security number on page 18 in this instruction book. (County is Trent and Length of Residence is 2 years and 6 months.)

f. Under Birth Date, write August 28, 1973.

g. Under No. of Dependents, write 1.

h. For Previous Residence, write N/A for "not applicable" because Tori has lived at her current residence longer than two years.

i. Refer to page 18 in this instruction book for information on Tori's employer and her salary. (Cabot's telephone number is 937-555-3777.)

j. For Previous Employer, write N/A because Tori has worked at her current job longer than two years.

k. For Name of Nearest Relative, list Chad Davis, 526 Stinson Road, Maplewood, OH 44920, 419-555-2510, father.

l. Under Checking/Savings Account, refer to Illustration 14 for Tori's checking account number. Her money market account is also with Hopewell Community Bank, account number 21-909090. (A *money market account* is a type of savings account in which the interest rate changes slightly from time

Phase Two   *Raising a Family*

to time. It tends to earn more interest than a regular account.)

m. The section on Credit Experience shows how much debt (or liabilities) Tori already has. This information is important to the bank. If Tori were already under heavy debt, she might not be able to pay back a car loan. The bank might then turn down her request.

In the first section, check Rent, write Lakeview Properties under Creditor, and write $700.00 under Monthly Payment. Skip the next two lines since Tori doesn't own property. Under Auto, write 1995 for Year and Tiara STX for Make of Auto. Be sure to write 0 under Balance and Monthly Payment to show that this car is paid for.

n. The last few lines are for all other debts and credit obligations. List Tori's WorldCard and the account number shown in Illustration 16. List $80.00 as the average monthly payment.

o. Sign Tori's signature and add the date. Tori would give the filled-out loan application to Alex, but you should file your copy behind the *Forms* tab in the file folder.

March 11

☐ 12. Tori and Carmen decide to eat dinner at Talia's, their favorite Italian restaurant. Tori pays the $28.60 bill, plus a $4.85 tip, with cash. Record the transaction in the *Financial Record Book* or computer file. Write the tip on the receipt (Form 39, page 89) so that you won't forget the amount you paid. Then file the receipt behind the *Receipts* tab in the file folder.

March 12

☐ 13. Tori stops at GasCo for gasoline again. Record the credit card transaction in the *Financial Record Book* or computer file, and file the receipt for $14.41 (Form 40, page 89) under *Receipts*.

March 14

☐ 14. Early in the evening, Tori and Carmen go shopping for groceries and a few other items. They stop at Fiori's Drug Store, because Carmen likes to visit with Mrs. Fiori. Tori pays $19.98 for sundries in cash. Then they go to Hilltop for groceries. Her bill there is $70.49, which she pays by using her debit card. Record the first transaction in the *Financial Record Book* or computer file only. Record the second transaction in the *Financial Record Book* or computer file and in the checkbook register. File the two receipts (Forms 41, page 89 and 42, page 91) under *Receipts*.

March 15

☐ 15. Since it looks like it's going to be a rainy day, Tori takes Carmen to The Children's Museum, where she can play with all sorts of exhibits and learning games. The tickets are $18.00, and their lunch is $13.45. Record these two cash payments in the *Financial Record Book* or computer file. File the tickets and the receipt (Forms 43 and 44, page 91).

March 17

☐ 16. Since today is the first working day after the 15th, Tori receives another receipt for the direct deposit of her paycheck. Check Form 45 (page 93) to make sure it's accurate before recording the deposit in the *Financial Record Book* or computer file and in the checkbook register. File the paycheck receipt under *Receipts*.

17. When Tori picks up Carmen at Stay & Play Child Care Center, she writes a check for $240.00 for the past two weeks of child care. Record the payment in the *Financial Record Book* or computer file and in the checkbook register. File the receipt (Form 46, page 93) under *Receipts*.

March 18

☐ **18.** At home, Tori goes online to the Web site of Books Etc. She owns a software package called BudgetXT, and she wants to learn how to use it to keep track of her finances electronically. She selects a book called *Getting Started with BudgetXT* for $25 and clicks the link labeled Add to My Shopping Cart. That's all she wants to buy, so she clicks Proceed to Checkout. The site sends her to a secure page that shows the amount of her purchase, including shipping, as $29.95. Following instructions at the site, she enters her e-mail address, mailing address, and credit card information. After checking that the information she entered is correct, she clicks Send to complete the transaction. Within minutes, she receives a receipt for her purchase by e-mail. Record the transaction under *Personal* in the *Financial Record Book* or computer file. Remember that credit transactions do not get recorded in the checkbook register until Tori pays the credit card bill by check. File the e-mail receipt (Form 47, p. 95) behind the *Receipts* tab.

19. Tori's monthly insurance bill (Form 48, page 97) is due on the 22nd. She carries three types of insurance with S&T Insurance Company: car, renter's, and life. Tori pays a monthly premium for each of these policies. She bought *renter's insurance* to cover her personal property, such as home furnishings and clothes, in case of loss from fire, theft, or other hazards at her rented condo. She carries a small amount of *life insurance* to provide funds to help care for Carmen if Tori died while Carmen was still young.

To pay the bill, Tori mails a check to S&T Insurance Company for $72.00. Record the check in the checkbook register. In the *Financial Record Book* or computer file, record the transaction on one line. However, divide up the total into the appropriate categories for each type of insurance. Refer to Form 48 and Tori's budget worksheet for guidance. File the receipt portion of the bill under *Receipts* and the bill portion under *Checks Written*.

March 19

☐ **20.** LaToya, one of the teachers at Stay & Play Child Care, calls Tori to say that Carmen has become sick at school. She has a high fever and is complaining that her ear hurts. Before leaving the office, Tori calls Carmen's doctor's office to make an appointment.

Tori picks up Carmen and takes her straight to Dr. Akita's office. Carmen is very patient while the doctor looks in her ears, eyes, and throat. Dr. Akita is sure that Carmen has an ear infection, so she writes two prescriptions for medicine.

Tori belongs to the health insurance plan offered by her employer. It is a network of doctors and health facilities called a *preferred provider organization (PPO)*. The plan will pay most medical expenses as long as Tori goes to doctors within the network. Tori's copayment for the doctor's visit is $15.00. At the drug store, her copayment for the prescriptions is $10.00 for each one, so she pays $20.00 for the medicine. Record two check payments in the *Financial Record Book* or computer file and in the checkbook register. File the receipts (Forms 49 and 50, page 99).

March 20

☐ **21.** Since Carmen is still not feeling well, Tori must stay home from work to take care of her. While Carmen is sleeping, Tori decides to revise her budget to see how much money she can afford for monthly car payments.

Retrieve her budget worksheet from the file folder, or open TMBUDGET on the data disk and save it as TMBUDGE2. Make the following revisions to Tori's budget as she finds ways to pull money from other categories to use for a car payment. Make the changes by crossing out the old amounts and writing in the new, or by replacing the figures in the spreadsheet cells in the computer file.

   a. Tori lowers her clothes and shoes limit to $180.00.

b. The new car shouldn't require as much maintenance, so she lowers that limit to $35.00.

c. Tori decides that she and Carmen can eat out less often and at less expensive restaurants, so she lowers that amount to $60.00.

d. Math check: Total the amount of money Tori is pulling from clothing and shoes, car maintenance, and restaurant meals. How much does Tori have for a monthly car payment so far?

   Suddenly, Tori realizes her car insurance premium might go up for a new car, so she calls her insurance agent, Mary Baker. Mary estimates that her insurance premiums will go up to about $70.00 monthly. This payment will require $25.00 more than she's spending now for insurance, so subtract that amount from your sum above. Now how much does Tori have to work with?

   Tori isn't sure how much her new car will cost, but she guesses that $175.00 a month will not be enough for a good new car, so she returns to her budget to make more changes.

e. As much as Tori enjoys the speed of a cable Internet connection, she decides to switch to a dial-up connection. The dial-up service will cost $22. The switch will save her $25 a month.

f. Next, Tori reduces her budget for event fees and tickets to $30.00.

g. Finally, she subtracts $20 from her allotment for gifts.

h. Math check: How much does Tori have for a car payment now? You should have arrived at $230.00. Enter this amount for Car Loan Payment under Transportation on the budget worksheet or file. Total the revised amounts in all budget categories to check that it still equals her net pay for the month.

22. Tori knows that one way she can keep her monthly car payments low is by paying as much as possible up front. The less money she borrows, the lower her payments will be. Tori decides to figure out how much money she can use for her *down payment* on the car.

Retrieve Tori's net worth form from the file folder, or open TMWORTH, to review her assets.

a. First, Tori will trade in her old car. She went online to the Kelley Blue Book Web site. After entering information about her car's model, year, mileage, features, and condition, she found that it is worth about $1,800.00.

b. Second, Tori looks at her savings account that she's been using to save money for a new car or other major purchase. She decides to leave some money in this account for emergencies, but she's willing to withdraw $3,500.00 for the down payment.

c. Tori briefly considers taking money from her 401(k) retirement account but decides it's better to leave that money alone. The financial penalty for withdrawing the money early would take a big bite out of her savings.

d. Math check: How much does Tori have for a down payment? You should have arrived at $5,300.00.

Now that Tori knows how much she has for a down payment and how much she can afford for monthly car payments, she can start shopping for a new car. In the meantime, she'll wait to hear whether her bank will approve a loan for her or whether she'll have to get a loan through the car dealership.

March 21

☐ **23.** Carmen is already feeling better, so Tori takes her to school and heads for the office. On the way, she stops for gasoline, once again using her credit card to pay the $13.85. Record the transaction in the *Financial Record Book* or computer file, and file the receipt (Form 51, page 101).

THINK IT THROUGH

1. Is shopping online safe? What steps can you take to safeguard your personal information while shopping online?
2. Review the description of good debt and bad debt on page 19. Do you think a car loan is good debt or bad debt? Do you think it's necessary to go into debt for a car?

March 22

☐ **24.** Tori and Carmen do their weekly grocery shopping. As usual, Tori uses her debit card to pay for the $62.14 in food and other items. Record the transaction in both records and file the receipt (Form 52, page 101).

25. Tori and Carmen stop at the video store and pick out a movie to rent. Tori pays the $4.98 rental fee in cash. She doesn't get a receipt, but she remembers to record the transaction when she gets home. Record the cash payment.

March 23

☐ **26.** Despite Tori's big purchase coming up in the near future, she must buy some new clothes for herself and for Carmen. She writes a check for $43.98 to pay for a new skirt from Donte's Dresses. She also writes a check for $28.45 for Carmen's new shoes from Shamrock Shoes. Finally, she writes a check to Peak Department Stores for $64.46 for some new clothes for Carmen. Record the transactions in both records and file the receipts (Forms 53, 54, and 55 on pages 101-103).

March 25

☐ **27.** Alex Littlebear, from Hopewell Community Bank, called yesterday to say that Tori's loan has been approved if she wants to use it. With this approval, she can start looking at cars tonight. But first, she and Carmen stop at Burger Express for a quick dinner. Record her cash payment of $9.82 in the *Financial Record Book* or computer file, and file the receipt (Form 56, page 103).

After dinner, Tori and Carmen stop at two car dealerships, one for new cars and one for used cars. At both places, the salespeople tell her that with a down payment of $5,300.00 and a five-year loan with monthly payments of $230.00 or less, she should be looking at cars in the $14,000 to $15,500 range. Tori decides her next step should be a trip to the library and the Internet to research new and almost-new cars in that price range.

March 26

☐ **28.** Tori receives her credit card bill from WorldCard. To keep her debt under control, she pays the entire balance on her credit card each month. Retrieve the three gas receipts and the receipt for her online purchase. Use them to make sure the bill is correct. If it is, write the total amount on the line next to *Payment Enclosed*. Then record a check for $73.45 in the checkbook register only. Since this payment represents credit transactions that have already been recorded in the *Financial Record Book* or computer file, do not deduct this amount there again. File the two portions of the bill (Form 57, page 105) behind the appropriate tabs in the file folder.

March 27

☐ **29.** Tori fills her car's gas tank at GasCo and charges the $13.72 to her credit card. Record the credit card payment and file the receipt (Form 58, page 107).

30. Tori stops for groceries at Hilltop. Her total is $67.14, which she pays with her debit card. Record the transaction and file the receipt (Form 59, page 107).

Phase Two   *Raising a Family*

March 28

☐ **31.** Because of all the planning, research, and shopping she is doing, Tori feels ready to buy a new car tomorrow. She would like to be prepared to buy a car as soon as she finds one that meets her requirements. So, she transfers $3,500.00 from her savings account into her checking account. Record this deposit in the *Financial Record Book* or computer file and in the checkbook register.

March 29

☐ **32.** This past week Tori went to the library to check out car-buying guides. She also spent several hours researching cars online. She read reviews of different models at car-oriented Web sites. At one site she compared prices and features of different models (Illustration 19). She also asked several friends and relatives for advice. She has narrowed her choices to three car models. She's decided to buy a used car if it is one of those three models, is no more than a year old, and has been driven less than 12,000 miles.

Tori's parents have agreed to watch Carmen for the day, so Tori heads for the car dealerships. By about 3:00 in the afternoon, she's decided which of the three types of car she wants, so she goes back to that dealership. They even have one used car that fits all her requirements. It happens to be the deluxe model of the car, but because it's a year old, it still fits within her price range. She and the car salesman, Bob Chen, negotiate a fair price for the car. Bob explains the loan options offered by the dealership, but Tori decides to use the loan from her own bank. It has the lowest interest rate. Once the paperwork is finished, Tori drives over to her parents' house in her new car.

Record a check for $3,500.00 to Trent County Auto Mall in the *Financial Record Book* or computer file and in the checkbook register. File the receipt (Form 60, page 109).

March 31

☐ **33.** When she picks up Carmen from daycare, Tori writes a check to Stay & Play Child Care Center for $240.00. Record the payment in the *Financial Record Book* or computer file and in the checkbook register. File the receipt (Form 61, page 109).

34. Later in the evening, Tori reconciles her checkbook. Unlike Ryan's bank, Tori's bank does not return the cancelled checks. Instead, Hopewell Community Bank sends just a statement (Form 62, page 111). Notice that this statement was prepared on 3/27, so any deposits made or checks cashed after that date will not be shown on this form. As you learned in Phase 1, *outstanding checks* are checks that have not yet finished their route through the banking system. As a result, Tori's bank has not yet subtracted the amounts from her checking account. Outstanding checks are one reason why the ending balance on your statement often doesn't agree with the ending balance in your checkbook register. To make sure your records and the bank's records are correct, then, you must reconcile the two.

Follow these steps to reconcile Tori's checkbook:

a. Compare all checks, deposits, online bill payments, and debit card transactions shown on the statement against the checkbook register. Check off each one that's correct. Like most banks, Hopewell lists the dates they paid the checks, not the dates the checks were written. The register should show one deposit and three outstanding checks that aren't shown on the statement.

b. To reconcile an account when the balance on the statement does not match the balance in the checkbook register, follow these steps on the back of the statement: On line 1, enter the closing balance shown on the bank statement.

c. In the spaces provided in part 2, record the deposit Tori made after the statement was prepared. Record the deposit total in the blank for line 2.

Phase Two   *Raising a Family*

Illustration 19: **Online Vehicle Comparison**

VEHICLE COMPARISON

[Pricing] [Features] [Specs]

PRICING

Pricing	Breeze Sedan	Red Hawk LT Sedan	Olympic S Sedan
Retail	$14,220	$15,292	$14,770
Invoice	$13,532	$14,276	$13,431
Destination Charge	$545	$575	$485
Warranty			
Basic	3 yr./36000 mi.	4 yr./50000 mi.	3 yr./36000 mi.
Drivetrain	5 yr./100000 mi.	5 yr./60000 mi.	5 yr./60000 mi.
Rust	5 yr./Unlimited mi.	12 yr./Unlimited mi.	5 yr./Unlimited mi.

FEATURES

	Breeze Sedan	Red Hawk LT Sedan	Olympic S Sedan
Base Engine Type & Cylinders	Inline 4	Inline 4	Inline 4
Base Engine Displacement	2.0 liters	2.0 liters	1.8 liters
Valvetrain	16 Valves double overhead cam (DOHC)	8 Valves single overhead cam (SOHC)	16 Valves double overhead cam (DOHC)
Horsepower	130 hp @ 5300 rpm	115 hp @ 5200 rpm	130 hp @ 6000 rpm
Torque	135 ft-lbs.@ 4500 rpm	122 ft-lbs. @ 2600 rpm	125 ft-lbs.@ 4200 rpm
4 Cyl	Standard	Standard	Standard
4 Speed Automatic	Optional	Not Available	Not Available
5 Speed Manual	Standard	Standard	Standard
Driven Wheels	Front wheel drive	Front wheel drive	Front wheel drive
Independent Suspension	Four-wheel	Four-wheel	Front
Stabilizer Bars	Front and rear	Front and rear	Front and rear
Tires	All season	All season	All season
Wheels	Alloy rims 16 in.	Steel rims 15 x 6 in.	Steel rims 16 x 6.5 in.
Spare	Spacesaver	Fullsize	Spacesaver
Front Wipers	Intermittent	Variable intermittent	Intermittent
Rear Wipers	Rear window wiper	Intermittent rear wiper	Intermittent rear wiper—optional
Rear Defogger	Standard	Standard	Standard
Privacy Glass	Standard	Not available	Not available
Total Seating Capacity	5	5	5
Front Seat Type	Sport	Bucket	Bucket
Upholstery Type	Premium cloth	Cloth	Cloth

Phase Two *Raising a Family*

d. Add the amounts in lines 1 and 2, and enter this subtotal in line 3.

e. In the spaces provided in part 4, list the three outstanding checks. Then add the amounts of the checks and enter the total in the blank for line 4.

f. Subtract line 4 from line 3, and enter this revised bank balance in line 5.

g. In line 6, enter the balance shown in the checkbook register. Next, enter the service charge and the interest shown on the bank statement. Follow the instructions in line 6 for adding and subtracting amounts, and enter the result in the blank for line 6.

h. Math check: The amounts on lines 5 and 6 should match. This is the true amount of money currently in the account: $775.01. If the amounts do not match, follow the advice at the bottom of the reconciliation form for checking your work.

i. The bank automatically withdraws a monthly fee of $4.00 from Tori's checking account for the online bill payment service. Record this service charge in the checkbook register. Record it under *Miscellaneous* in the *Financial Record Book*.

j. The bank pays Tori interest for keeping her money in their bank. Record the interest shown on the statement, $4.26, as a deposit in the checkbook register and in the *Financial Record Book*. The checkbook register should now show a balance of $775.01, the same ending balance shown on the reconciliation form.

35. Math check: Before proving cash in the *Financial Record Book* or computer file, test your math skills by reconstructing Tori's cash transactions to determine how much cash she has left.

Add the amount of Tori's remaining cash to the ending balance in your checkbook register. You may think that this total should match the ending balance in your *Financial Record Book* or computer file, as it did in Ryan's case. But it doesn't match. In fact, this balance should be $13.72 higher than the balance in the *Financial Record Book*. Can you figure out why?

It's because Tori charged $13.72 for gasoline to her credit card, which has already been deducted from the balance in the *Financial Record Book*. However, she hasn't paid the credit card company yet, so the amount hasn't been deducted from her checking account balance. This fact explains the difference in the two balances.

36. As the last step, total each of the payment columns (both pages) in the *Financial Record Book* or computer file. Write your answers in the boxes at the bottom of each column on the second page.

THINK IT THROUGH

1. Pretend that you have used a credit card to purchase $800.00 worth of items. You will have to pay off your debt at an interest rate of 15%. Also pretend that you have $900.00 in a savings account that earns 3% interest. Should you use the savings to pay off the debt?

2. Continuing with this story, pretend that you don't have any money in savings. But you plan to pay off the debt by making $100.00 payments each month until the debt is gone. What changes might happen in your life that would make this plan difficult to carry out?

3. What effect, if any, will Tori's new car have on her net worth?

Investing in the Future

Phase 3

KEISHA AND JAMAL BOOKER

Thirty-two-year-old Keisha Booker has been married to Jamal Booker, also 32, for eight years. Shortly after marrying, they bought a small house. Their address is 402 Stanton Drive, Maplewood, OH 44922. Their telephone number is (419) 555-9113.

Keisha is a registered nurse. She's worked at the Maplewood Hospital for six years. Her social security number is 912-65-0018. Her annual salary is $42,500.00. About three years ago, Jamal started his own business, Booker Computer Services. Jamal installs and repairs personal computers in homes and small businesses. He enjoys working for himself, but he's had to work very hard and put in many hours to make his business a success. He estimates that he'll earn about $44,000.00 this year. His social security number is 076-45-5013.

Keisha and Jamal would like to buy a somewhat larger house. Lately, they've been thinking that in addition to purchasing a new home, they should begin saving for retirement. They will need to find ways to meet these financial goals. Although they've budgeted for expenses and savings since they were married, they want to use the money they're earning more wisely. They're sure that their saved money could be earning more money if it were invested in something other than low-interest savings accounts. They need both a short-term plan and a long-term plan for how to use their money in the future.

Performance Outcomes

In the last phase of this simulation, you will learn to:

1. Prepare a statement of net worth and a budget for a married couple.
2. Estimate federal income taxes for a self-employed person.
3. Find a reliable financial planner.
4. Investigate various ways to use your money to earn money, including real estate purchases, retirement savings plans, mutual funds, and stocks.
5. Understand the purpose of different kinds of insurance.
6. Fill out a home loan qualifying application.
7. Continue developing sound financial practices involving recordkeeping, decision making, and planning.

Special Topic: How Your Money Can Earn More Money

Do you recall reading about paying interest on loans and credit cards (see "Credit Showdown," page 19 in this instruction book)? Interest is the additional amount you pay for the use of someone else's money, right? In a similar way, your money can earn interest for you when you loan it to others so they can use it. Let's say you have money that you're not using for monthly expenses or saving for a particular purpose or an emergency. It's smart to loan this extra money to someone else so that the money can make more money—earn interest—for you. Loaning money this way is called *investing*.

Of course, you wouldn't want to loan your money to just anybody. Two trustworthy groups you may lend money to are banks and investment companies. These two groups need money to conduct their business, and they're willing to pay you interest for the privilege of using your money to do it. However, investing involves risk. **Risk** is the chance that your investment may lose value. If the bank or investment company uses your money for something that loses, rather than earns, money, you may not be able to get your money back.

Risk is an important concept to understand, because it influences how you'll decide to invest your money. In general, low-risk investments are "sure things," which means that you're very likely to get your money back. It also means, though, that you won't earn much interest. On the other hand, high-risk investments have the potential to pay you lots of money in interest—or to cost you lots of money if the deal "goes bad" and your money is lost. When you're young, you can afford to take higher risks, because you have time to earn back the money if you lose it. However, older people generally want to stick with safe, low-risk investments.

Here are just a few of the many types of investments you can make:

- **Certificates of deposit (CDs).** You agree to loan your money to a bank for a certain amount of time (usually six months to five years). The bank agrees to pay you an interest rate that is slightly higher than a savings account. However, if you withdraw your money from the CD before the term is up, you will have to pay a financial penalty. CDs are a low-risk investment.
- **Bonds.** You agree to loan your money to an organization for up to 30 years for a specific rate of interest. To get your money out, you can sell your bonds at any time. However, the amount you earn overall depends on the value of the bonds at the time you sell. Typically, bonds are a low-risk investment.

- **Stocks.** You agree to invest your money in a corporation by buying small portions of it. These portions are called *shares*. If you own shares of stock, you are a *stockholder*, or part-owner of the corporation. If the company grows and increases in profits, you get a part of those profits in the form of *dividends*. Stocks vary widely in the risk involved, depending on the company.
- **Real estate.** You agree to buy a piece of property, but you let someone else live in or use it. You earn money from the rent that person pays you. Real estate investments involve a wide range of risk, depending on what kind of property it is and to whom you're renting.
- **Mutual funds.** You agree to invest in a fund, generally a collection of stocks and bonds that are chosen by the fund manager. You earn your share of dividends and interest from the fund's stocks and bonds. Mutual funds can be low risk or high risk, depending on the risk level of the stocks and bonds in the collection.

You can get your money out of stocks and mutual funds by selling your shares and out of real estate by selling the property. Like bonds, if you can sell these investments for more than you paid for them, then you have earned a profit in addition to the interest or rent. However, if you sell at a time when the value of your investment is below the price you paid, you will lose part of the money you invested.

Why is it so important for you to invest money and let your extra income earn more money for you? It's not so you can go out and buy more clothes and video games. You want to earn as much as you can because throughout your lifetime, you will probably want to buy some big, expensive things, such as a house or a college education for yourself, your spouse, and/or your children. You'll also want to save money for your retirement, so you'll have money to live on when you're no longer earning an income. These things are so expensive that many people can't afford them on just their income from their jobs. Investing helps you achieve your long-term financial goals by giving you another source of income.

FIGURING OUT THE BOOKERS' NET WORTH

Determine Keisha and Jamal's net worth by retrieving Form 63 (page 113 of this instruction book) or by calling up the NETWORT3 file on the data disk. Refer to the directions on page 3 in this instruction book if needed.

Assets

- $6,922.82 in a checking account.
- $11,140.21 in a savings account.
- $8,800.00 in certificates of deposit.
- Current value of their house, $125,000.
- Current value of their two cars, $17,100.00.
- Value of their personal items, $3,800.00.
- $165.00 in cash.

Phase Three *Investing in the Future*

Liabilities

- Mortgage, $95,200.00
- Universal Cellular phone bill, $27.45
- Tri-County Gas & Electric bill, $112.28.
- Pilot Internet Connections payment due, $21.95
- TDS Satellite TV bill, $39.99
- Car loans, $11,946.00.
- Homeowner's insurance, $47.50.
- Annual car registration fee (for Keisha), $55.00.
- Income tax (for Jamal), $2,770.00.
- Property tax, $1,650.00.

Math check: Be sure to check your math before filing Form 63 in the *Forms* section or saving this file as KJWORTH.

WRITING OUT THE BOOKERS' BUDGET

Begin by retrieving Form 64 (page 113 in this instruction book) or calling up BUDGET from the template disk. Use the figures below to fill out the Bookers' worksheet.

The Bookers' Budget Information

Monthly Income
Gross Pay, $7,208.00
Taxes/Deductions, $1,037.70
Net Pay, $6,170.30

Savings/Debt Payoff
Savings Accounts, $2,224.30

Home
Mortgage Payment, $830.00
Property Tax, $275.00
Utilities, $176.00
Cell Phone Service, $30.00
Satellite TV Service, $40.00
Internet Service, $22.00
Home Maintenance, $60.00
Homeowner's Insurance, $48.00

Food/Sundries
Food, $280.00
Personal Care Items, $90.00
Small Home Care Items, $45.00

Personal
Clothes and Shoes, $275.00
Haircuts/Salon Services, $70.00

Transportation
Car Loan Payments, $457.00
Car Insurance, $240.00
Gasoline/Oil, $100.00
Car Maintenance, $120.00
License/Registration Fees, $10.00

Entertainment
Restaurant Meals, $175.00
Event Fees/Tickets, $90.00
Travel Expenses, $350.00

Miscellaneous
Gifts, $80.00
Bank Service Charges, $3.00

Health Care
Doctor and Dental Fees, $35.00
Prescription Medicines, $20.00
Glasses/Contact Lenses, $25.00

Math check: Total your entries in all categories to make sure your sum matches the Bookers' combined monthly net pay.

File the Bookers' budget worksheet under *Forms* or save the document as KJBUDGET.

Once again, you will work through one month's worth of financial transactions. Check the box as you complete each day's activities.

APRIL TRANSACTIONS

April 1

☐**1.** On the first page of the *Financial Record Book* for Phase 3, enter the Bookers' total amount of spendable money (checking account balance plus cash shown on their net worth statement). Enter the date as 4/1, record the description as Opening Balance, and enter the amount in the *Balance* column. Or, open FINREC on your template disk, record the opening balance, and save the document as KJAPRIL.

Start a new page in the checkbook register and enter the Bookers' checking account balance in the first Balance Fwd box.

2. Jamal makes a mortgage payment on the first of each month. In fact, he usually pays all of their bills before they're due. He doesn't want their credit rating damaged by late payments. Just as you did in Phase 2, you will record all checking account transactions in the *Financial Record Book* and checkbook register, without actually writing checks or deposit tickets. Record a payment of $830.00 to State Bank of Ohio in the *Financial Record Book* or computer file and in the checkbook register (check #1312). File the mortgage payment receipt (Form 65, page 115) under *Checks Written*.

April 2

☐**3.** On her way home from work, Keisha stops at Capital Service Station to put gasoline in her car. At this gas station, she's able to use her debit card to pay for the gas. Record a debit card payment of $15.25 in the *Financial Record Book* or computer file and in the checkbook register. File the receipt (Form 66, page 115) under *Receipts*.

4. Next, Keisha stops at Family Foods for grocery shopping. Record another debit card payment of $67.94 in the *Financial Record Book* or computer file and in the checkbook register. File the receipt (Form 67, page 115) under *Receipts*.

April 3

☐**5.** One of Keisha's co-workers, Armando, is retiring soon, so Keisha stops at a shop called Small Treasures to buy a gift. Record a check for $21.28 in the *Financial Record Book* or computer file and in the checkbook register. File the receipt (Form 68, page 117) under *Receipts*.

April 4

☐**6.** Keisha and Jamal invite Keisha's parents to dinner at Ryan Davis's restaurant, the Crossroads Inn. As they're enjoying their meal, Jamal mentions that he and Keisha are seriously thinking of moving to a bigger house, just in case they decide to have children in the future. Keisha's parents agree that buying a house is a good investment, but her father suggests that Keisha and Jamal look into other types of investments, too. Her mother also suggests that the couple find a professional financial planner who can help them plan the best ways to spend and invest their money.

Record a cash payment of $87.05 plus a tip of $15.00 in the *Financial Record Book* or computer file. Write the amount of the tip on the receipt (Form 69, page 117) and file the receipt.

April 5

☐**7.** Because Jamal works for himself, no money is withheld from his paychecks for income taxes. Therefore, he has to handle his income taxes in a special way. *Self-employed* people are required to estimate their income for the current year and figure the income tax they would owe on this income. Then they make partial payments on the tax four times a year (quarterly), starting April 15. Since this deadline is coming soon, Jamal figures his estimated tax for the year so that he'll know how much tax to pay now.

Begin by removing Form 70 from page 119. Form 1040-ES is used to figure estimated taxes. Jamal will be filing with the IRS as a married person filing a separate tax form from Keisha, since his income tax is paid quarterly and hers is paid through her employer throughout the year.

a. Jamal estimates that his adjusted gross income (income + taxable interest from savings) will be $44,275.00. Enter this amount on line 1.

b. Jamal decides to use the standard deduction, which is $3,975.00 for a married person filing separately. Enter this amount on line 2.

c. Follow the directions for line 3.

d. Jamal takes only one exemption, so enter the appropriate amount on line 4.

e. Follow the directions for line 5 to find Jamal's taxable income.

f. Using the tax chart (Illustration 20), find Jamal's income tax on Schedule Y-2. This amount is determined by adding $3,258.75 + 27% of the difference between his taxable income—$37,250.00—and $23,725.00. Here are the calculations:

$37,250.00 $13,525.00 $3,651.75
−23,725.00   ×   .27   +3,258.75
$13,525.00 $ 3,651.75 $6,910.50

Enter $6,910.50 on line 6.

g. Since line 7 doesn't apply to Jamal, record 0 on that line and transfer the amount from line 6 to line 8.

h. Line 9 also doesn't apply to Jamal. Record 0 on line 9 and follow the instructions for line 10.

i. In the blank space within the line 11 instructions, record the amount Jamal expects to earn this year: $44,000. Since this amount is less than $87,000, multiply his expected earnings, $44,000, by 15.3%. (Note that his interest income is

Illustration 20: Estimated Income Tax Chart

Tax Rate Schedules

Caution. Do not use the Tax Rate Schedules to figure this year's taxes. Use only to figure next year's estimated taxes.

Single—Schedule X

If line 5 is: Over—	But not over—	The tax is:	of the amount over—
$0	$ 6,000	.... 10%	$0
6,000	28,400	$600.00 + 15%	6,000
28,400	68,800	3,960.00 + 27%	28,400
68,800	143,500	14,868.00 + 30%	68,800
143,500	311,950	37,278.00 + 35%	143,500
311,950	....	96,235.50 + 38.6%	311,950

Head of household—Schedule Z

If line 5 is: Over—	But not over—	The tax is:	of the amount over—
$0	$10,000	.... 10%	$0
10,000	38,050	$1,000.00 + 15%	10,000
38,050	98,250	5,207.50 + 27%	38,050
98,250	159,100	21,461.50 + 30%	98,250
159,100	311,950	39,716.50 + 35%	159,100
311,950	....	93,214.00 + 38.6%	311,950

Married filing jointly or Qualifying widow(er)—Schedule Y-1

If line 5 is: Over—	But not over—	The tax is:	of the amount over—
$0	$12,000	.... 10%	$0
12,000	47,450	$1,200.00 + 15%	12,000
47,450	114,650	6,517.50 + 27%	47,450
114,650	174,700	24,661.50 + 30%	114,650
174,700	311,950	42,676.50 + 35%	174,700
311,950	....	90,714.00 + 38.6%	311,950

Married filing separately—Schedule Y-2

If line 5 is: Over—	But not over—	The tax is:	of the amount over—
$0	$ 6,000	.... 10%	$0
6,000	23,725	$600.00 + 15%	6,000
23,725	57,325	3,258.75 + 27%	23,725
57,325	87,350	12,330.75 + 30%	57,325
87,350	155,975	21,338.25 + 35%	87,350
155,975	....	45,357.00 + 38.6%	155,975

Phase Three *Investing in the Future*

not included as it was on line 1.) Enter the result on line 11.

j. Since there are no other taxes, record 0 on line 12. Add lines 10 and 11 and enter the sum on line 13a.

k. Jamal can't take the earned income credit or additional child tax credit, so record 0 on line 13b. Transfer the amount from line 13a to line 13c.

l. Follow the directions for line 14a.

m. Jamal's income tax for last year was $11,080.00. Enter that amount on line 14b.

n. Follow the directions for line 14c. This amount is the total estimated tax Jamal will pay on his income for this year. He must divide this total by four and pay it in quarterly amounts called *installments*. At the end of the year he will figure the actual tax he owes when he fills out his tax return. At that time he will pay any additional tax he owes or will receive a tax refund if he paid too much in estimated installments.

o. Since Jamal doesn't withhold anything from his paychecks, record 0 on line 15 and transfer the amount from line 14c to line 16.

p. Follow the directions for line 17 to find out how much tax Jamal should pay in each installment. When the installment amount has cents, Jamal always rounds up to the nearest dollar to make sure he pays at least the minimum required to avoid a penalty.

Jamal's final step is to write a check to the United States Treasury for his first installment. He mails the check, along with a special form called a *payment voucher* (Illustration 21), to the Internal Revenue Service (IRS). Record a check for $2,770.00 to the United States Treasury in the *Financial Record Book* or computer file under Savings/Debt Payoff and in the checkbook register. File Form 70 (Form 1040-ES) under *Forms*. Note that Jamal will have to make this $2,770.00 payment every three months. Therefore, he should establish a habit of setting aside a third of this total each month ($924.00) under Savings/Debt Payoff (budget subcategory Other) to save for the rest of the income tax installments this year.

Math check: Your answers should be: line 11—$6,732.00; line 13a—$13,642.50; line 14a—$12,278.25.

Illustration 21: Payment Voucher for First Estimated Tax Installment

April 7

☐ **8.** Keisha and Jamal would like to spend a day working in the yard. They both enjoy gardening, and they want their house to look nice, especially if they're going to sell it. So, they go to Sumida's Lawn and Garden Shop, where Mr. Sumida helps them choose yard equipment. Record a check for $43.57 in the *Financial Record Book* or computer file and in the checkbook register. File the receipt (Form 71, page 121).

April 8

☐ **9.** Keisha and Jamal stop at Family Foods for more groceries. Record a debit card payment for $72.32 in the *Financial Record Book* or computer file and in the checkbook register. File the receipt (Form 72, page 121).

April 9

☐ **10.** It's time for Jamal to pay some bills. He goes to his bank's Web site and enters his user ID and PIN to log in. He then clicks the links to the bill payment page. Jamal enters the following payments: Universal Cellular, $27.45; Tri-County Gas & Electric, $112.28; and TDS Satellite TV, $39.99. Record these online payments in the *Financial Record Book* or computer file and in the checkbook register. File the receipt portions of the bills (Forms 73, 74, and 75, pages 123-127) under *Receipts* and the bill portions under *Checks Written*.

April 10

☐ **11.** Keisha and Jamal think that finding a financial planner is a good idea. Although they could research their investment options on their own, they know it would use up much of their free time. Also, they'd prefer to have an expert's opinion. So for the past several days, they've been visiting Web sites of financial magazines, banks, investment companies, and consumer-oriented organizations to learn more about financial planning and investing. They've also been checking the telephone book and online for names of financial planners and asking friends for recommendations. They've discovered they have many choices.

Several local banks and investment companies have *certified financial planners* on staff. These investment professionals are trained to help clients achieve their financial goals through sound planning and investing. Some financial planners are paid on commission. This means that they receive a small portion of the profits your investments earn. Other financial planners charge a flat fee for each hour of financial review and advice. Keisha and Jamal have decided to work with Marta Reyes, who charges a flat fee of $110.00 an hour.

First, Marta looks over the Bookers' statement of net worth, their monthly budget, and their financial record. Next, she asks them to define their goals. They tell her that their goals are to buy a larger house soon and to save for retirement. Marta asks the couple many detailed questions about these goals and then makes several recommendations:

a. **Pay off the car loans**. The Bookers have two car loans, both of which have rather high interest rates, near 10%. Paying off the loans sooner will save them money because they won't have to pay as much interest.

b. **Contribute to a 401(k) or an IRA**. Marta says that saving even a little more of their salaries each month will make a big difference in the total at retirement. To make her point, she shows them a chart of the total savings with 401(k) contributions of 6% of salary compared to 3% (Illustration 22). Keisha can participate in her employer's 401(k) plan. Since Jamal's business has no retirement plan, he can set up an *individual retirement account (IRA)*. Not only are retirement accounts a great way to invest and earn interest, but they also provide a "tax break." Money put into either a 401(k) or a traditional IRA is *tax-deferred income*. Jamal and Keisha wouldn't have to pay income tax now on money deposited into such accounts. The taxes are put off, or "deferred," until the funds are withdrawn at retirement age. A *Roth IRA* offers a different kind of tax break. Jamal and Keisha would have to pay taxes on the income they contribute now, but they wouldn't pay taxes when they withdraw the money. This means that the earnings on the Roth IRA funds are never taxed.

Illustration 22:
401(k) Earnings Potential Chart

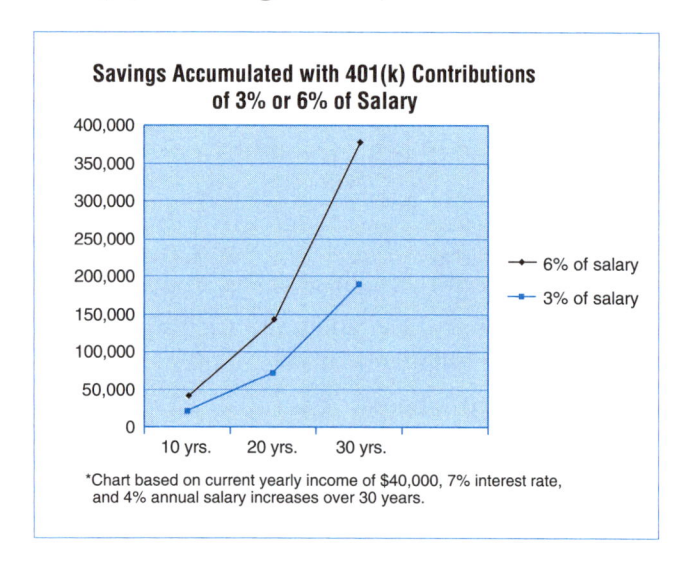

Savings Accumulated with 401(k) Contributions of 3% or 6% of Salary

Chart based on current yearly income of $40,000, 7% interest rate, and 4% annual salary increases over 30 years.

c. **Purchase a term life insurance policy on Jamal**. Keisha already has life insurance as a *fringe benefit* of her job. But if Jamal died suddenly, Keisha would have a difficult time meeting her financial obligations without his income. Marta recommends buying a *term life insurance* policy that would pay Keisha $500,000.00 if Jamal died within the 20-year time period, or "term," that the policy is in force.

d. **Invest in mutual funds**. Although Marta approves of keeping a sizable amount in savings for emergencies, she also thinks that the extra income the Bookers earn in the future should be invested in mutual funds. She explains that mutual funds *diversify* or spread the risk among the stocks and bonds of many organizations. If the Bookers bought stock in just a few individual companies, their entire investment would depend on the performance of those few companies. With mutual funds, the collection is so large that if some of the stocks lose value, others will likely gain value, offsetting the losses.

e. **Buy a new home**. One good reason for Keisha and Jamal to buy a new house is that interest rates on mortgages are lower now than they were when they bought their current house. Thus, they could get a slightly more expensive house by borrowing money at a lower interest rate and still make about the same monthly payments as they do now.

An alternative to moving to a new house would be to *refinance* their current mortgage. This means they would take out a new mortgage at a lower interest rate to pay off the current high-interest mortgage. Refinancing can require large fees, so the Bookers would have to make sure the interest rate would be low enough to make paying the fees worthwhile.

All told, Keisha and Jamal spent about two-and-a-half hours in this meeting. Record a check for $275.00 to Marta Reyes in the *Financial Record Book* or computer file under Miscellaneous and in the checkbook register. File the receipt (Form 76, page 129).

Phase Three *Investing in the Future*

THINK IT THROUGH

1. If you need information or advice on financial matters, where could you go for help?
2. Based on the information in Illustration 22, how old do you think a person should be to start saving and investing for retirement?
3. What is *risk* in investing, and how would it affect your investment choices?

April 11

☐ 12. Jamal and Keisha stop at Capital Service for gasoline. Record a debit card payment of $14.11 in the *Financial Record Book* or computer file and in the checkbook register. File the receipt (Form 77, page 129).

13. Keisha's car registration fee is due. Record a check for $55.00 to the Ohio Department of Motor Vehicles in the *Financial Record Book* or computer file and in the checkbook register. File the receipt portion of Form 78 (page 131) under *Receipts*, and file the outgoing portion under *Checks Written*.

April 13

☐ 14. Based on the financial planner's advice, the Bookers have decided to start putting money in Keisha's 401(k) account. She can put in a maximum of 6% of her income, and her employer, Maplewood Hospital, will contribute 50 cents to her account for each dollar she saves.

To see how Keisha joins the 401(k) plan, retrieve Form 79 from page 133. Follow along as Keisha and Jamal fill out this enrollment form.

  a. Use the following information to complete the top portion. Name: Keisha Booker. Social security number: 912-65-0018. Birthdate: 1/8/1972. Marital status: married.
  b. For question 1, write 6%, since Keisha and Jamal want to contribute the maximum amount possible.
  c. For question 2, Keisha and Jamal must decide how to divide the money they contribute to the 401(k) account among these six investment options. The options are ranked in order of risk. The first option has the lowest risk and will likely earn the lowest interest. The last option has the most risk but also the highest earning potential. Because they want to increase their assets and they're young enough to afford to take some risks, they decide to put 10% in option 3, 30% in option 4, 40% in option 5, and 20% in option 6. Math check: Their choices should total 100%.
  d. Of course, Jamal is the Spouse Primary Beneficiary in question 3. Keisha and Jamal choose Keisha's parents, Darnell and Taryn Moore, as their Non-spouse Primary Beneficiaries in question 4.
  e. Keisha signs and dates the form and gives it to the employee benefits specialist at the hospital. The specialist says the contributions will begin with her next paycheck.

File the form in the file folder.

April 14

☐ 15. Once again, Keisha stops at Family Foods for groceries. Record a debit card payment of $64.71 in the *Financial Record Book* or computer file and in the checkbook register. File the receipt (Form 80, page 135).

16. At home, Keisha checks her e-mail and finds a receipt from Pilot Internet Connections. Last month at Pilot's Web site, she signed up for the *automatic bill payment* program. To get started, she filled out an online form that included her name, address, phone number,

e-mail address, and credit card number. Now, Pilot automatically charges the monthly Internet connection fee to her WorldCard and sends her an e-mail receipt of the transaction. Record the $21.95 credit card transaction in the *Financial Record Book* or computer file. (Remember that charge payments aren't recorded in the checkbook register until the credit card bill is paid.) File the e-mail receipt (Form 81, page 135) under *Receipts*.

April 15

☐ 17. Jamal goes online to compare prices for $500,000, 20-year term life insurance policies. He fills out online applications for quotations from five insurance companies. *Quotations* are written descriptions of the terms and prices of the policies offered. Before choosing a company, Jamal goes to the library to check the company's rating in *Best's Insurance Reports*, published by the A.M. Best Company. He wants to make sure the insurance company has a good track record for paying *claims*. He and Keisha decide to buy a policy from Secure-One Life Insurance Company. The *premiums* (payments) will be $420.00 each year for the next 20 years. Record a check for $420.00 in the *Financial Record Book* or computer file under Personal and in the checkbook register.

18. Record the direct deposit of Keisha's paycheck for $1,251.98 in the *Financial Record Book* or computer file and in the checkbook register. (Assume that Keisha received a paycheck receipt for this direct deposit.)

April 16

☐ 19. Keisha and Jamal have decided to repaint their kitchen, so they go to Goldberg's Hardware for paint and brushes. Record a check for $86.09 in the *Financial Record Book* or computer file and in the checkbook register. File the receipt (Form 82, page 137).

20. Jamal and Keisha also have another kind of insurance, called *homeowner's insurance*. It will help pay for replacing stolen possessions or repairing damage to their house caused by fire, storms, or other hazards. Record a check for $47.50 to PaxCo Insurance Co. in the *Financial Record Book* or computer file and in the checkbook register. File the two portions of Form 83 (page 137) in the appropriate places.

April 18

☐ 21. Keisha must buy special medical clothing called scrubs to wear on her job. She stops at Donna's Uniforms and picks out a new set of scrubs. Record a check for $31.74 in the *Financial Record Book* or computer file and in the checkbook register. File the receipt (Form 84, page 139).

April 19

☐ 22. Keisha's sister Monique calls to invite Keisha and Jamal to join her and a friend for dinner and a play on the 24th. Monique and her friend already have their tickets. Keisha immediately calls the theater box office to reserve tickets for herself and Jamal. Record a WorldCard payment of $55.00 to Pinetree Playhouse in the *Financial Record Book* or computer file. Do not record it in the checkbook register until the credit card bill is paid. When Keisha and Jamal pick up their tickets at the theater on the night of the play, the ticket stubs will become the receipts.

April 20

☐ 23. Two years ago, the Bookers had deposited $1,500.00 in a two-year certificate of deposit. Now that the two-year term is up, they must decide what to do with the money. They could *roll over*, or reinvest, the money into a new CD. Instead, they decide to invest it in a mutual fund that Jamal has researched through the Internet and in financial magazines. This particular fund is made up of several steadily

Phase Three *Investing in the Future*

growing stocks and has been earning an average interest rate near 10% for the past three years.

Jamal fills out a simple application form (much like Form 79), showing how he wants to invest the money. He then sends the application and a check for $1,500.00 to the company that manages the mutual fund, Foster & Stern Investments. Record both a deposit of $1,500.00 (from the CD) and a $1,500.00 check in the *Financial Record Book* or computer file and in the checkbook register. In a few weeks, and every three months after that, Jamal will receive a report showing how much money this investment is earning.

THINK IT THROUGH

1. If the Bookers were 20 years older than they are now, would it change the way they decided to divide the 401(k) investment? Give an example of the way a couple in their 50s might split their contributions, using the six investment options on Form 79.

2. Throughout this simulation, you have learned about several types of insurance. Name three types of insurance, and tell why each is important.

April 21

☐ **24.** Jamal is running errands. He stops to pick up some groceries at Family Foods. Record a debit card payment of $47.82 in the *Financial Record Book* or computer file and in the checkbook register. File the receipt (Form 85, page 139).

25. Next, Jamal stops at Capital for gas. Record a cash payment of $12.72 in the *Financial Record Book* or computer file. File the receipt (Form 86, page 139).

April 24

☐ **26.** Jamal and Keisha have agreed to meet Monique and her friend at La Maison, a local French restaurant. Jamal wants to be sure they have enough cash to pay for dinner, so he stops at the bank first. He uses his debit card to withdraw $60.00 from their checking account. Record the withdrawal in the checkbook register but not in the *Financial Record Book* or computer file since he hasn't actually spent the money yet. File the ATM receipt (Form 87, page 141).

27. Keisha and Jamal enjoy having dinner with Monique and her friend at La Maison. Record a cash payment of $48.50 plus a tip of $8.50 in the *Financial Record Book* or computer file. Write the amount of the tip on the receipt (Form 88, page 141). Then file the receipt.

28. File the theater ticket stubs (Form 89, page 141) under *Receipts*.

April 25

☐ **29.** Jamal must go for his annual eye examination. Under a special eye care insurance policy through Keisha's job, Jamal will pay only $30.00 for the exam. The doctor says that since his eyes haven't changed in the past year, he doesn't have to buy new glasses. Record a check to Dr. Heather Byrd in the *Financial Record Book* or computer file and in the checkbook register. File the receipt (Form 90, page 143).

April 26

☐ **30.** Jamal pays both car loans. Record one check for $216.40 to State Bank of Ohio and one check for $240.60 to Oak Grove Bank in the *Financial Record Book* or computer file and in the checkbook register. File the payment slips that would accompany the checks (Forms 91 and 92, pages 143-145) under *Checks Written*. Next month, Jamal will arrange a new payment plan with his bank so he can increase the amount of his payments and pay off these debts faster.

April 27

❑ **31.** Jamal stops at a convenience store for a few personal care items. Record a check for $11.11 to Corner Mart in the *Financial Record Book* or computer file and in the checkbook register. File the receipt (Form 93, page 145).

April 28

❑ **32.** Once every six months, Jamal and Keisha must pay their property taxes. Because the amount is rather large, they set aside $275.00 each month. Setting money aside enables them to pay the bill when it's due. Record a check for $1,650.00 to the City of Maplewood in the *Financial Record Book* or computer file and in the checkbook register. File the two portions of the bill (Form 94, page 147) in the appropriate sections of the file folder.

April 29

❑ **33.** Keisha and Jamal have continued to discuss their many investment options. In addition to opening the 401(k) account and putting money in a mutual fund, they've decided to put their house up for sale and look for a larger house.

Keisha goes to their bank to get a home loan qualifying application. This form is not a true loan application, but rather a preliminary form to find out if they will qualify for a home loan. Retrieve Form 95 from page 149 and follow along as Keisha fills out the form.

a. Using information from the introduction to this phase, fill out as much of the top portion as you can. Keisha will be the Applicant, and Jamal will be the Co-Applicant. Keisha's work phone is 419-555-3200 and business address is 225 Chase Street, Maplewood, OH 44922. Jamal's work phone is 419-555-9178, and his business address is their home address.

b. Based on your knowledge of the Bookers, answer the questions under Eligibility Requirements.

c. Use the information in the introduction to fill in their annual salaries in the Income Information section.

d. Use the checkbook register to fill in the amount currently in their checking account. To fill in their other Assets, use the information given for determining the Bookers' net worth. Remember that the $1,500.00 that used to be in a CD is now in a mutual fund. Math check: The checkbook register should show $924.64 in their checking account at this point.

e. Under Liabilities, fill in their Mortgage Payment ($830.00). Although they pay off their credit card bill each month, Jamal estimates that they charge an average of $100 on the card each month. Record $100 for Credit Card Debt. For Other Loans, fill in the total of their two monthly car payments shown in their budget ($457.00).

f. Sign and date the form as if you were both Keisha and Jamal.

Keisha will return this form to the bank, but you can file it under *Forms*.

34. Record the direct deposit of Keisha's paycheck for $1,145.73 in the *Financial Record Book* or computer file and in the checkbook register. Notice that Keisha's net pay is less than it was the last time because of her 401(k) contribution (Illustration 23). Also record a deposit of $3,700.00 for Jamal's earnings for the month.

Illustration 23: Keisha's Paycheck Receipt Showing Her 401(k) Contribution

Maplewood Hospital

225 Chase Street
Maplewood, OH 44922
(419) 555-3200

Direct Payroll Deposit

Employee:

Keisha Booker
402 Stanton Drive
Maplewood, OH 44922

(419) 555-9113

SSN: 912-65-0018

Payroll Period: 4/15/-- to 4/30/--

Gross Pay:	$1,770.83
Deductions:	
401(k)	$ 106.25
Federal	301.04
Social Security	100.94
State	49.58
Medicare	31.87
Health Insurance	35.42
Net Pay:	$1,145.73

Deposited to: #334-067214

---

35. Using Form 96 (page 151), reconcile the Bookers' checking account. Since this statement was prepared on April 28, there will be four outstanding checks and two outstanding deposits not shown on this statement. This account was charged a fee of $3.00 and doesn't earn any interest. Refer to the directions for reconciling Tori's checking account on page 33 in this instruction book if you need help. After reconciling the account, be sure to record the service charge in the *Financial Record Book* or computer file and in the checkbook register.

36. To prove cash in the *Financial Record Book*, you must first reconstruct the Bookers' cash transactions. Math check: You should have arrived at $53.23 cash remaining.

Using this information and your final checking account balance, prove cash in the *Financial Record Book* or computer file. Math check: Remember that the two ending balances will be $76.95 apart because the two credit card transactions have not yet been paid by check.

Refer to the directions for proving Tori's cash on page 35 in this instruction book if you need help. Be sure to enter the column totals at the bottom of the second page of the *Financial Record Book*.

Phase Three *Investing in the Future*

THINK IT THROUGH

1. Did Keisha and Jamal go over their spending limit in any of the budget subcategories? If so, how might they accommodate this difference?

2. Name five principles of smart financial management you have learned during the course of this simulation.

3. As an optional exercise, you may want to challenge yourself by revising Keisha and Jamal's budget based on their investment decisions. A clean worksheet (Form 97, page 153) has been provided for this exercise. Because of the 401(k) account contributions, their total net income for each month is now $5,957.80. Create a plan that will allow for a larger mortgage payment and a larger car payment. Plan a monthly set-aside of $35.00 to cover the $420 annual life insurance premium ($420/12 months = $35). Also plan a monthly income tax set-aside of $924.00 (listed under Savings/Debt Payoff/Other). This monthly tax set-aside is needed to cover Jamal's $2,770.00 installment due every three months ($2,770.00/3 = $924.00 rounded up). Then decide how much to devote to savings and/or other investments, and adjust the other categories if you think it's needed.

Phase Three *Investing in the Future*

STATEMENT OF NET WORTH FOR _____

Form 1

Assets	Liabilities and Net Worth
Checking Account	Car Loan ....
Savings Account	Rent Due ....
Savings Bond	Gas/Electric Bill ....
Car	Phone Bill ....
Personal Items	Total Liabilities ....
Cash	Net Worth ....
Total Assets	Total Liabilities and Net Worth ...

BUDGET WORKSHEET FOR _____

Form 2

Monthly Income

Gross Pay .... _____
Taxes/Deductions .... _____
Net Pay .... _____

Monthly Expenses

Savings/Debt Payoff .... _____
Savings Accounts .... _____
Investments .... _____
Loan Payments .... _____
Other (_____) _____

Home .... _____
Rent/Mortgage Payment ..... _____
Property Taxes .... _____
Utilities .... _____
Phone/Pager Services .... _____
Cable/Satellite TV Service .... _____
Internet Service .... _____
Home Maintenance .... _____
Home/Renter's Insurance ..... _____
Home Furnishings .... _____
Home Electronics .... _____

Food/Sundries .... _____
Food .... _____
Personal Care Items .... _____
Small Home Care Items .... _____

Personal .... _____
Clothes & Shoes .... _____
Haircuts/Salon Services .... _____
Dry Cleaning/Laundry .... _____
Gym Membership .... _____
Life Insurance .... _____

Transportation .... _____
Car Loan Payment .... _____
Car Insurance .... _____
Gasoline/Oil .... _____
Car Maintenance .... _____
License/Registration Fees ..... _____
Bus/Subway Fares .... _____

Entertainment .... _____
Restaurant Meals .... _____
Event Fees/Tickets .... _____
Travel Expenses .... _____

Miscellaneous .... _____
Child Care Expenses .... _____
Gifts .... _____
Donations/Charities .... _____
Pet/Hobby Expenses .... _____
Education Fees .... _____
Bank Service Charges .... _____

Health Care .... _____
Doctor & Dental Fees .... _____
Prescription Medicines .... _____
Glasses/Contact Lenses .... _____

Column 1 Total .... _____   **Column 2 Total** .... _____
                                              Grand Total .... _____

STATEMENT OF NET WORTH FOR _____

Form 26

Assets		Liabilities and Net Worth	
Checking Account		Rent Due	
Savings Account		Gas/Electric Bill	
401(k) Account		Phone Bill	
Life Insurance Policy		Cable TV & Internet	
Car		Insurance Bill	
Personal Items		Total Liabilities	
Cash		Net Worth	
Total Assets		Total Liabilities and Net Worth	

BUDGET WORKSHEET FOR _____

Form 27

Monthly Income
Gross Pay .... _____
Taxes/Deductions .... _____
Net Pay .... _____

Monthly Expenses

Savings/Debt Payoff .... _____
Savings Accounts .... _____
Investments .... _____
Loan Payments .... _____
Other (_____) _____

Home .... _____
Rent/Mortgage Payment ..... _____
Property Taxes .... _____
Utilities .... _____
Phone/Pager Services .... _____
Cable/Satellite TV Service .... _____
Internet Service .... _____
Home Maintenance .... _____
Home/Renter's Insurance .... _____
Home Furnishings .... _____
Home Electronics .... _____

Food/Sundries .... _____
Food .... _____
Personal Care Items .... _____
Small Home Care Items .... _____

Personal .... _____
Clothes & Shoes .... _____
Haircuts/Salon Services .... _____
Dry Cleaning/Laundry .... _____
Gym Membership .... _____
Life Insurance .... _____

Transportation .... _____
Car Loan Payment .... _____
Car Insurance .... _____
Gasoline/Oil .... _____
Car Maintenance .... _____
License/Registration Fees ..... _____
Bus/Subway Fares .... _____

Entertainment .... _____
Restaurant Meals .... _____
Event Fees/Tickets .... _____
Travel Expenses .... _____

Miscellaneous .... _____
Child Care Expenses .... _____
Gifts .... _____
Donations/Charities .... _____
Pet/Hobby Expenses .... _____
Education Fees .... _____
Bank Service Charge .... _____

Health Care .... _____
Doctor & Dental Fees .... _____
Prescription Medicines .... _____
Glasses/Contact Lenses .... _____

Column 1 Total .... _____   **Column 2 Total** .... _____
Grand Total .... _____

Form 28

Cabot Services, Inc.

8820 Main Street
Hopewell, OH 45311
(937) 555-3777

Tori Davis-Martinez
4388 Canal Street
Hopewell, OH 45313
SSN: 111-55-9999

Direct Deposit Paycheck Receipt
(This is not a check.)

Date Issued: 3/1/--

Amount Deposited: $1,347.23

Pay	This Period	YTD
Gross Pay	$1,750.00	$7,000.00
Net Pay	$1,347.23	$5,388.92

Deductions	This Period	YTD
401(k)	$ 70.00	$280.00
Federal Tax	$180.60	$722.40
State Tax	$ 31.39	$125.56
Soc. Sec.	$ 59.45	$237.80
Medicare	$ 21.33	$ 85.32
PPO Health Plan	$ 40.00	$160.00

Deposited to:
Hopewell Community Bank
Checking account #: 21-436587

Form 29

Easy-Fix Car Care

DATE: 3/3   TIME: 12:15

OIL CHANGE	32.99
AIR FILTER	18.69
SUBTOTAL	51.68
TAX	3.10
TOTAL	54.78

Form 30

Tori Davis-Martinez
4388 Canal Street
Hopewell, OH 45313

Acct. No. 227–7A
Amount Due $95.10
Date Due 3/7/--

TCG&E

Tri-County Gas & Electric
P.O. Box 13579
Maplewood, OH 44920

Detach and return this portion with your payment.

BILLING EXPLANATION

BILLING PERIOD	ITEM	CURRENT CHARGES
2/1 – 2/28	Gas Meter #6389	$33.11
	Electricity Meter #83114A	$61.99

Questions? Please call 419-555-4679 for service.

TRI-COUNTY GAS & ELECTRIC

Form 31

PBC Telephone Co.

Tori Davis-Martinez
4388 Canal Street
Hopewell, OH 45313

Account No. 1-937-555-2262
Amount Due by 3/8/-- $44.31

PBC Telephone Co.
Dept. 2581
Hopewell, OH 45313

File this portion with your records.

Last Month
Previous Bill Amount $42.85
Payment Received $42.85
Last Month's Balance .... $ 0.00

This Month
Monthly Service $25.07
Monthly Maintenance .... $ 2.00
Federal Tax .... $ .75
Long Distance Service $16.49

Total Due $44.31

PBC Telephone Co.

You can rely on us!

77

Form 32

Express
Cable Service

Customer:

Tori Davis-Martinez
4388 Canal Street
Hopewell, OH 45313

Express Cable Service
23 S. Third Street
Hopewell, OH 45313

Keep this statement for your records.

Basic Television Service $39.53
E-Express Internet Service $46.72
Tax $ 0.70

Amount Due: $86.95
Date Due: 3/12/--

Express
Cable Service

Stay tuned for **special offers** on premium channels next month!

Form 33

GasCo

Date: 3/6
Station: 618
Pump: 2

Regular Gas $15.24

Charged to WorldCard **** 9867

Save this receipt for your records.

79

Form 34

THANK YOU FOR SHOPPING
HILLTOP GROCERY STORE

STACI WAS YOUR CASHIER.   TIME   5:52
DATE 3/6

CEREAL   4.25
PARMESAN CHEESE   4.12

BREAD   2.79
LUNCHMEAT   3.29
MILK   2.99
GR BEEF   2.31
1.01 LB @ 2.29/LB

SUBTOTAL $78.15
*TAX $1.18
TOTAL $79.33
DEBIT $79.33

Form 35

JASON'S GARAGE

15692 FIFTH ST., HOPEWELL, OH 45313
(937) 555-8020

CUSTOMER NAME:	TORI DAVIS-MARTINEZ	PHONE:	555-2262
CAR MAKE: TIARA	MODEL: STX		YEAR: 1995

SERVICE ESTIMATE

LABOR – 3 HRS @ $50/HR	$150.00
PARTS	$35.00
CUSTOMER'S INITIAL: TDM	$185.00

TOTAL DUE	
TOTAL PAID	

Form 1040A — Department of the Treasury—Internal Revenue Service
U.S. Individual Income Tax Return (99) 20--   IRS Use Only—Do not write or staple in this space.

OMB No. 1545-0085

Label (See page 21.)

Use the IRS label. Otherwise, please print or type.

L A B E L   H E R E

Your first name and initial | Last name | Your social security number

If a joint return, spouse's first name and initial | Last name | Spouse's social security number

Home address (number and street). If you have a P.O. box, see page 22. | Apt. no.

City, town or post office, state, and ZIP code. If you have a foreign address, see page 22.

▲ **Important!** ▲ You **must** enter your SSN(s) above.

Presidential Election Campaign (See page 22.)
Note. Checking "Yes" will not change your tax or reduce your refund.
Do you, or your spouse if filing a joint return, want $3 to go to this fund? ▶
You: ☐ Yes ☐ No   Spouse: ☐ Yes ☐ No

Filing status
Check only one box.

1 ☐ Single
2 ☐ Married filing jointly (even if only one had income)
3 ☐ Married filing separately. Enter spouse's SSN above and full name here. ▶ _____
4 ☐ Head of household (with qualifying person). (See page 23.) If the qualifying person is a child but not your dependent, enter this child's name here. ▶ _____
5 ☐ Qualifying widow(er) with dependent child (year spouse died ▶ ___). (See page 24.)

Exemptions

6a ☐ **Yourself.** If your parent (or someone else) can claim you as a dependent on his or her tax return, **do not** check box 6a.
b ☐ **Spouse**
c **Dependents:**

If more than six dependents, see page 24.

(1) First name Last name	(2) Dependent's social security number	(3) Dependent's relationship to you	(4) ✓ if qualifying child for child tax credit (see page 25)
			☐
			☐
			☐
			☐
			☐
			☐

No. of boxes checked on 6a and 6b ___
No. of children on 6c who:
• lived with you ___
• did not live with you due to divorce or separation (see page 26) ___
Dependents on 6c not entered above ___
Add numbers on lines above ☐

d Total number of exemptions claimed.

Income

Attach Form(s) W-2 here. Also attach Form(s) 1099-R if tax was withheld.

If you did not get a W-2, see page 27.

Enclose, but do not attach, any payment.

7 Wages, salaries, tips, etc. Attach Form(s) W-2. | 7
8a Taxable interest. Attach Schedule 1 if required. | 8a
b Tax-exempt interest. **Do not** include on line 8a. 8b
9 Ordinary dividends. Attach Schedule 1 if required. | 9
10 Capital gain distributions (see page 27). | 10
11a IRA distributions. 11a | 11b Taxable amount (see page 27). | 11b
12a Pensions and annuities. 12a | 12b Taxable amount (see page 28). | 12b
13 Unemployment compensation and Alaska Permanent Fund dividends. | 13
14a Social security benefits. 14a | 14b Taxable amount (see page 30). | 14b
15 Add lines 7 through 14b (far right column). This is your **total income.** ▶ | 15

Adjusted gross income

16 Educator expenses (see page 30). | 16
17 IRA deduction (see page 30). | 17
18 Student loan interest deduction (see page 33). | 18
19 Tuition and fees deduction (see page 33). | 19
20 Add lines 16 through 19. These are your **total adjustments.** | 20
21 Subtract line 20 from line 15. This is your **adjusted gross income.** ▶ | 21

For Disclosure, Privacy Act, and Paperwork Reduction Act Notice, see page 57.   Cat. No. 11327A   Form **1040A** (20--)

Form 1040A (20--) Page 2

Form 36

Tax, credits, and payments	22	Enter the amount from line 21 (adjusted gross income).	22	
	23a	Check if: ☐ **You** were 65 or older ☐ Blind / ☐ **Spouse** was 65 or older ☐ Blind — **Enter number of boxes checked** ▶ 23a ☐		
	b	If you are married filing separately and your spouse itemizes deductions, see page 34 and check here ▶ 23b ☐		
Standard Deduction for—	24	Enter your **standard deduction** (see left margin).	24	
• People who checked any box on line 23a or 23b **or** who can be claimed as a dependent, see page 34.	25	Subtract line 24 from line 22. If line 24 is more than line 22, enter -0-.	25	
	26	Multiply $3,000 by the total number of exemptions claimed on line 6d.	26	
	27	Subtract line 26 from line 25. If line 26 is more than line 25, enter -0-. This is your **taxable income.** ▶	27	
	28	**Tax,** including any alternative minimum tax (see page 35).	28	
• All others: Single, $4,700	29	Credit for child and dependent care expenses. Attach Schedule 2.	29	
Head of household, $6,900	30	Credit for the elderly or the disabled. Attach Schedule 3.	30	
Married filing jointly or Qualifying widow(er), $7,850	31	Education credits. Attach Form 8863.	31	
	32	Retirement savings contributions credit. Attach Form 8880.	32	
	33	Child tax credit (see page 38).	33	
Married filing separately, $3,925	34	Adoption credit. Attach Form 8839.	34	
	35	Add lines 29 through 34. These are your **total credits.**	35	
	36	Subtract line 35 from line 28. If line 35 is more than line 28, enter -0-.	36	
	37	Advance earned income credit payments from Form(s) W-2.	37	
	38	Add lines 36 and 37. This is your **total tax.** ▶	38	
	39	Federal income tax withheld from Forms W-2 and 1099.	39	
	40	20-- estimated tax payments and amount applied from 20-- return.	40	
If you have a qualifying child, attach Schedule EIC.	41	**Earned income credit (EIC).**	41	
	42	Additional child tax credit. Attach Form 8812.	42	
	43	Add lines 39 through 42. These are your **total payments.**	43	
Refund	44	If line 43 is more than line 38, subtract line 38 from line 43. This is the amount you **overpaid.**	44	
Direct deposit? See page 52 and fill in 45b, 45c, and 45d.	45a	Amount of line 44 you want **refunded to you.** ▶	45a	
	▶b	Routing number ☐☐☐☐☐☐☐☐☐ ▶ c Type: ☐ Checking ☐ Savings		
	▶d	Account number ☐☐☐☐☐☐☐☐☐☐☐☐☐☐☐☐☐		
	46	Amount of line 44 you want **applied to your 20-- estimated tax.** 46		
Amount you owe	47	**Amount you owe.** Subtract line 43 from line 38. For details on how to pay, see page 53. ▶	47	
	48	Estimated tax penalty (see page 53). 48		

Third party designee Do you want to allow another person to discuss this return with the IRS (see page 54)? ☐ **Yes.** Complete the following. ☐ **No**

Designee's name ▶   Phone no. ▶ (   )   Personal identification number (PIN) ▶ ☐☐☐☐☐

Sign here
Under penalties of perjury, I declare that I have examined this return and accompanying schedules and statements, and to the best of my knowledge and belief, they are true, correct, and accurately list all amounts and sources of income I received during the tax year. Declaration of preparer (other than the taxpayer) is based on all information of which the preparer has any knowledge.

Joint return? See page 22.
Keep a copy for your records.

Your signature	Date	Your occupation	Daytime phone number ( )
Spouse's signature. If a joint return, **both** must sign.	Date	Spouse's occupation	

Paid preparer's use only

Preparer's signature ▶	Date	Check if self-employed ☐	Preparer's SSN or PTIN
Firm's name (or yours if self-employed), address, and ZIP code ▶		EIN Phone no. ( )	

Form **1040A** (20--)

84

JASON'S GARAGE

15692 FIFTH ST., HOPEWELL, OH 45313
(937) 555-8020

Form 37

CUSTOMER NAME: TORI DAVIS-MARTINEZ	**PHONE:** 555-2262	
CAR MAKE: TIARA	**MODEL:** STX	**YEAR:** 1995

ESTIMATE

LABOR – 3 HRS @ $50/HR	$150.00
PARTS	$ 35.00
CUSTOMER'S INITIAL: TDM	$185.00

SERVICE

LABOR – 3 HRS @ $50/HR	$150.00
ACTUAL PARTS	$ 40.00
SUBTOTAL	$190.00
TAX	$ 11.40

TOTAL DUE	$201.40
TOTAL PAID	$201.40

Hopewell Community Bank

Credit/Loan Application

Branch _____

Form 38

Purpose (This application may NOT be used for either a line of credit secured by residential real estate or a variable rate installment loan secured by principal residence.)

Amount Requested _____ Terms Requested _____

Applicant Information

Last Name	First Name	Mid. Initi. Suffix
(Business Loan Only) Business Name		
Address		
Address		
City	State/ZIP Code	
County	Length of Residence Years Months	
Phone	Social Security No.	
Birth Date	No. of Dependents	
Previous Residence (If less than 2 years)		
City	State/ZIP Code	
Length of Residence Years Months		

Employer	
Occupation	
Phone	Length Employed Years Months
Previous Employer (If less than 2 years)	
Occupation	
Phone	Length Employed Years Months
Gross Salary	Weekly (W) Bimonthly (B) Monthly (M) Annually (A) (circle one)
Other Income (circle one) W B M A	Source
Name of Nearest Relative Not Living With You	
Address	
Phone	Relationship

Checking/Savings Accounts

Bank Name	Account Number	Account Type
Bank Name	Account Number	Account Type

Credit Experience/Obligations
(i.e., include all existing payments such as credit cards, department stores, bank or finance co. loans, and other obligations such as alimony, child support or separate maintenance, guarantees or co-maker on loans.)

Creditor	Account Number	Balance	Monthly Payment	To Be Paid Off With This Loan (Yes/No)
( ) Mortgage ( ) Rent ( ) Other				
Second Mortgage/ Home Equity				
If Real Estate Owned: Date of Purchase	Purchase Price		Current Market Value	
Auto Year of Auto Make of Auto				
Auto Year of Auto Make of Auto				

If I do not qualify for credit with you, I authorize you to consider my application under the terms and conditions of any applicable alternative loan program. Such loan may be sold to another lender with which you have a relationship. I authorize you to forward my application and other documentation to that lender and understand that the terms and conditions may differ from those for which I am currently applying.

☐ I am not interested in having my application considered for an alternative loan program.

Applicant's Signature _____ Date _____

Form 39

Talia's
Fine Dining

Date: 3/11
Time: 6:57

Dinner	$14.99
Child's Dinner	$ 7.99
Drink	$ 2.50
Child's Drink	$ 1.50
Subtotal	$26.98
Tax	$ 1.62
Total	$28.60
Amount Given	$30.00
Change Due	$ 1.40

Form 40

GasCo

Date: 3/6
Station: 618
Pump: 8

Regular Gas $14.41

Charged to WorldCard **** 9867

Save this receipt for your records.

Form 41

Fiori's
Drug Store

PANTYHOSE	2.25
PANTYHOSE	2.25
DEODORANT	1.97
FACIAL TISSUE	2.89
GREETING CARD	3.10
GREETING CARD	3.10
MAGAZINE	3.29
SUBTOTAL	18.85
TAX	1.13
TOTAL DUE	19.98
AMOUNT GIVEN	20.00
CHANGE DUE	.02

Form 42

THANK YOU FOR SHOPPING
HILLTOP GROCERY STORE

DATE 3/14   TIME 7:36

SPAGHETTI   1.29
GREEN BEANS   1.42
 0.89 LB @ 1.59/LB

BANANAS   .72
 1.05 LB @ .69/LB
COFFEE   5.99
TUNA   5.48
 2 @ 2.74

        SUBTOTAL $69.51
        *TAX $.98
        TOTAL $70.49
        DEBIT $70.49

Form 43

THE CHILDREN'S MUSEUM
ADMIT 1 ADULT
DATE: 3/15   PRICE: $10.00

THE CHILDREN'S MUSEUM
ADMIT 1 CHILD
DATE: 3/15   PRICE: $8.00

Form 44

Welcome to
THE CHILDREN'S MUSEUM Restaurant

SANDWICH ---------- $4.50
HOT DOG ----------- $3.25
FRUIT ------------- $1.49
DRINK ------------- $1.15
CHIPS ------------- $1.15
DRINK ------------- $1.15
        ---------- SUBTOTAL $12.69
        ---------- TAX $ .76
        ---------- TOTAL $13.45
        ---------- AMOUNT PAID $13.45

THANK YOU! COME AGAIN!

Form 45

Cabot Services, Inc.

8820 Main Street
Hopewell, OH 45311
(937) 555-3777

Tori Davis-Martinez
4388 Canal Street
Hopewell, OH 45313
SSN: 111-55-9999

Direct Deposit Paycheck Receipt
(This is not a check.)

Date Issued: 3/15/--

Amount Deposited: $1,347.23

Pay	This Period	YTD
Gross Pay	$1,750.00	$8,750.00
Net Pay	$1,347.23	$6,736.15

Deductions	This Period	YTD
401(k)	$ 70.00	$350.00
Federal Tax	$180.60	$903.00
State Tax	$ 31.39	$156.95
Soc. Sec.	$ 59.45	$297.25
Medicare	$ 21.33	$106.65
PPO Health Plan	$ 40.00	$200.00

Deposited to:
Hopewell Community Bank
Checking account #: 21-436587

Form 46

Receipt   Date: 3/17/--

Issued By: Stay & Play Child Care Center
For: Child Care for 3/1 – 3/15
Amount: $240.00 by check
From: Tori Davis-Martinez (Carmen)
Signed: Nicole Quinn

93

Tori Davis-Martinez

From: auto-confirm@booksetc.com
Sent: March 18, 20—
To: tmartinez@expresslink.com
Subject: Your Order with Books Etc.

Books Etc.

[VIEW CART] [YOUR ACCOUNT] [HELP]

Thanks for your order, Tori!

Purchase Information:

E-mail Address: tmartinez@expresslink.com

Billing Address:
Tori Davis-Martinez
4388 Canal Street
Hopewell, OH 45313
United States
(937) 555-2262

Shipping Address:
Tori Davis-Martinez
4388 Canal Street
Hopewell, OH 45313
United States
(937) 555-2262

Purchase Total $29.95

Order Summary:

Shipping Details
Order #: 076-23801
Shipping Method: Standard
Subtotal of Items: $25.00
Shipping & Handling: $ 4.95
Total for This Order: $29.95

Shipping estimate: March 19, 20—
Delivery estimate: March 26, 20—

1   **"Getting Started with BudgetXT"**
      Luis Fuentes; paperback; $25.00

Tori Davis-Martinez
4388 Canal Street
Hopewell, OH 45313

Due: 3/22/--

Amount: $72.00

S&T

S&T Insurance Company
PO Box 276
Columbus, OH 43218

Policy Number	Coverage	Monthly Premium
TDM 373 AUTO	Car Insurance	$45.00
TDM 477 RENT	Renter's Insurance	$15.00
TDM 880 LIFE	Whole Life Insurance	$12.00

Return this portion with your payment.

TDM 373 AUTO	$45.00	
TDM 477 RENT	$15.00	
TDM 880 LIFE	$12.00	
TOTAL	**$72.00**	

Due: 3/22/--

S&T Insurance Company
PO Box 276
Columbus, OH 43218

Tori Davis-Martinez
4388 Canal Street
Hopewell, OH 45313

Form 49

Dr. Isako Akita, M.D.
Pediatrician
231 Shane Drive, Suite 4
Hopewell, OH 45311
(937) 555-2727

Date: 3/19   Time: 3:25

Patient's Name: CARMEN MARTINEZ

Patient Number: CM - 238

Patient's Address: 4388 CANAL STREET, HOPEWELL

Diagnosis: EAR INFECTION

Copayment: $15.00

Paid: $15.00 BY CHECK (T. DAVIS-MARTINEZ)

Signed: *Susan Franks*

Form 50

Fiori's Drug Store

PRESCRIPTION #1	10.00
PPO PLAN	
PRESCRIPTION #2	10.00
PPO PLAN	
TOTAL DUE	20.00
CHECK GIVEN	20.00

Form 51

GasCo

Date: 3/21
Station: 618
Pump: 5

Regular Gas $13.85

Charged to WorldCard   **** 9867

Save this receipt for your records.

Form 52

THANK YOU FOR SHOPPING
HILLTOP GROCERY STORE

TAMEKA WAS YOUR CASHIER.
DATE 3/22   TIME 1:15

LUNCH BAGS*	.78
PAPER TOWELS*	1.19
BREAD	2.79
FRZN JUICE	1.09
SOUR CREAM	1.88
DELI LUNCHMEAT	3.85
TOILET PAPER*	3.77
STRAWBERRIES	1.95
1 PINT	

SUBTOTAL	$61.42
*TAX	$ .72
TOTAL	$62.14
DEBIT	$62.14

Form 53

Donte's Dresses

SKIRT	$41.49
#3131 4680 921	
SUBTOTAL	$41.49
TAX	$2.49
TOTAL	$43.98
CHECK GIVEN	$43.98

*Fine Dresses, Suits,
& Casual Clothing*

Form 54

Shamrock Shoes
Where Kids Come First

Date: 3/23
Time: 2:06

Shoes	$16.99
Sandals	$9.85

Subtotal	$26.84
Tax	$1.61
Total	$28.45
Amount Paid	$28.45
Balance Due	$0.00

Form 55

*P*eak
Department Stores

Today's Date   3/23

CHILD'S DRESS Item #12114	$22.98
CHILD'S DRESS Item #12830	$14.29
CHILD'S T-SHIRT Item #12872	$ 9.99
CHILD'S PANTS Item #12661	$13.55

SUBTOTAL	$60.81
6% TAX	$ 3.65
TOTAL	$64.46
PAID	$64.46

Refunds & Exchanges
Require Receipt

Form 56

```
BURGER EXPRESS

KID'S MEAL....  3.99
BURGER........  3.29
SM FRIES......   .99
SM DRINK......   .99

SUB...........  9.26
TAX...........   .56
TOT...........  9.82
PAID.......... 10.00
CHG...........   .18

       THANK YOU
```

Form 57

CUSTOMER NAME: Tori Davis-Martinez	DATE DUE: 3/31/--
CUSTOMER CARD #: 0000 4321 0000 9867	BALANCE: $73.45
	MINIMUM PAYMENT: $10.00
	PAYMENT ENCLOSED: _____

WORLDCARD

WORLDCARD
36216 AVENUE OF THE AMERICAS
NEW YORK, NY 10126

RETURN THIS PORTION WITH YOUR PAYMENT.

Tori Davis-Martinez   ACCOUNT NO. 0000 4321 0000 9867

DATE	DESCRIPTION	REFERENCE NUMBER	AMOUNT
3/6	GasCo	75420TR	$15.24
3/12	GasCo	69998BC	$14.41
3/18	Books Etc. (www.booksetc.com)	29666SR	$29.95
3/21	GasCo	42325DK	$13.85
		TOTAL	$73.45

WORLDCARD

For Customer Service, call 555-263-7422

Form 58

GASCO

Date: 3/27
Station: 618
Pump: 1

Regular Gas $13.72

Charged to WorldCard   **** 9867

Save this receipt for your records.

Form 59

THANK YOU FOR SHOPPING
HILLTOP GROCERY STORE

DAVID WAS YOUR CASHIER.
DATE 3/27   TIME   6:11

PORK CHOPS   4.12
  0.96 LB @ 4.29/LB
SHAMPOO*   3.45
ALUM FOIL*   2.75
COOKIES   3.29

GALA APPLES   1.20
  1.04 LB @ 1.15/LB
TOILET PAPER*   3.77
BAGELS   2.58
  2 @ 1.29

    SUBTOTAL $65.04
    *TAX $2.10
    TOTAL $67.14
    DEBIT $67.14

Form 60

Trent County Auto Mall (937) 555–AUTO   BILL OF SALE

Salesperson: Bob Chen Date: 3/29/--	List Price — 16,500	00
Customer: Tori Davis-Martinez	Purchase Price — 15,200	00
Address: 4388 Canal Street Hopewell, OH 45313	Document Fees — 40	00
Home Phone: 937-555-2262 Bus. Phone: 937-555-3777	Subtotal — 15,240	00

Trade-In
Make: Tiara   Model: STX Sedan   Mileage: 98,678

Car Purchased   [ ] New   [X] Used
Make: Olympic   Model: S-Class Sedan   Mileage: 11,081

Features
- [ ] Manual Transmission
- [X] Automatic Transmission
- [X] Anti-lock Brakes
- [X] Driver-side Air Bag
- [X] Passenger Air Bag
- [X] Air Conditioning
- [ ] Standard Sound System
- [X] Deluxe Sound System
- [X] Power Windows
- [X] Power Locks
- [ ] Sun Roof
- [X] Floor Mats

6% Sales Tax	914	40
State & Local Fees	155	25
Total Price	16,309	65
Trade-in Allowance	1,800	00
Partial Payment	3,500	00
Balance	11,009	65

Financing   Bank: Hopewell Community Bank
Amount: $11,009.65   Loan Approval #: 21-339214

Bob Chen
DEALER'S SIGNATURE

Tori Davis-Martinez
CUSTOMER SIGNATURE

3/29/--
DATE

Form 61

Receipt .... Date: 3/31/--

Issued By: Stay & Play Child Care Center
For: Child Care for 3/16 – 3/31
Amount: $240.00 by check
From: Tori Davis-Martinez (Carmen)
Signed: Nicole Quinn

109

Hopewell Community Bank

Tori Davis-Martinez
4388 Canal Street
Hopewell, OH 45313

Statement prepared on:	3/27/--
Opening Balance:	$339.27
Closing Balance:	$1,088.46
Account Number:	21-436587

Checks

Check No.	Date Paid	Amount
672	3/5	54.78
673	3/6	700.00
674	3/11	201.40
675	3/19	240.00
676	3/21	72.00

Check No.	Date Paid	Amount
677	3/23	15.00
678	3/22	20.00
679	3/25	43.98
680	3/26	28.45
681	3/27	64.46

Debits and Withdrawals

Date	Amount	Description
3/4	95.10	Online payment: Tri-County Gas & Electric
3/4	44.31	Online payment: PBC Telephone Co
3/4	86.95	Online payment: Express Cable Service
3/6	79.33	Debit transaction: Hilltop Grocery
3/14	70.49	Debit transaction: Hilltop Grocery
3/22	62.14	Debit transaction: Hilltop Grocery
3/27	67.14	Debit transaction: Hilltop Grocery
3/27	4.00	Service Charge: Online Bill Payment Service

Deposits

Date	Amount	Description
3/2	1,347.23	Direct Payroll Deposit: Cabot Services
3/17	1,347.23	Direct Payroll Deposit: Cabot Services
3/27	4.26	Interest Earned

HOPEWELL COMMUNITY BANK

Account Reconciliation Form

1. Enter closing balance from statement. $ _____

2. List deposits/credits made after statement date:

DATE	AMOUNT	DATE	AMOUNT	DATE	AMOUNT

Enter total of above deposits and credits. $ _____

3. Compute subtotal (#1 plus #2). $ _____

4. List checks, withdrawals, and debits not yet paid by bank:

CHECK NO. OR DATE	AMOUNT	CHECK NO. OR DATE	AMOUNT	CHECK NO. OR DATE	AMOUNT

Enter total of above checks, withdrawals, and debits. $ _____

5. Enter revised bank balance (#3 minus #4). $ _____

6. Enter checkbook balance $ _____
   Subtract service charges $ _____
   Add interest paid $ _____
   Enter result $ _____

Final amount on Line 6 should be the same as your revised bank balance on Line 5. If not, please consult section below.

If revised bank balance is MORE than your checkbook balance:	If revised bank balance is LESS than your checkbook balance:
(a) Have you checked your addition and subtraction above and in your checkbook?	(a) Have you checked your addition and subtraction above and in your checkbook?
(b) Does the above list include all of your outstanding checks, withdrawals, and debits?	(b) Have you deducted service and other bank charges in your checkbook?
(c) Have you added all ATM deposits in your checkbook?	c) Have you deducted all ATM withdrawals in your checkbook?
(d) Have you added all credits and advances in your checkbook?	(d) Have you deducted all credit line and preauthorized payments in your checkbook?

In case of errors or questions about your account, call (937) 555-6000.

STATEMENT OF NET WORTH FOR _____

Form 63

Assets

Checking Account	
Savings Account	
CDs	
Home	
Cars	
Personal Items	
Cash	
Total Assets	

Liabilities and Net Worth

Mortgage	
Phone Bill	
Gas/Electric Bill	
Internet Service Bill	
Satellite TV Bill	
Car Loans	
Home Insurance	
Car Registration	
Income Tax	
Property Tax	
Total Liabilities	
Net Worth	
Total Liabilities and Net Worth	

BUDGET WORKSHEET FOR _____

Form 64

Monthly Income

Gross Pay .... _____
Taxes/Deductions .... _____
Net Pay .... _____

Monthly Expenses

Savings/Debt Payoff .... _____
Savings Accounts .... _____
Investments .... _____
Loan Payments .... _____
Other (_____) .... _____

Home .... _____
Rent/Mortgage Payment ..... _____
Property Taxes .... _____
Utilities .... _____
Phone/Pager Service .... _____
Cable/Satellite TV Service ... _____
Internet Service .... _____
Home Maintenance .... _____
Home/Renter's Insurance ... _____
Home Furnishings .... _____
Home Electronics .... _____

Food/Sundries .... _____
Food .... _____
Personal Care Items .... _____
Small Home Care Items ..... _____

Personal .... _____
Clothes & Shoes .... _____
Haircuts/Salon Services ..... _____
Dry Cleaning/Laundry .... _____
Gym Membership .... _____
Life Insurance .... _____

Transportation .... _____
Car Loan Payment .... _____
Car Insurance .... _____
Gasoline/Oil .... _____
Car Maintenance .... _____
License/Registration Fees ... _____
Bus/Subway Fares .... _____

Entertainment .... _____
Restaurant Meals .... _____
Event Fees/Tickets .... _____
Travel Expenses .... _____

Miscellaneous .... _____
Child Care Expenses .... _____
Gifts .... _____
Donations/Charities .... _____
Pet/Hobby Expenses .... _____
Education Fees .... _____
Bank Service Charges .... _____

Health Care .... _____
Doctor & Dental Fees .... _____
Prescription Medicines .... _____
Glasses/Contact Lenses ..... _____

Column 1 Total .... _____ **Column 2 Total** .... _____
Grand Total .... _____

Form 65

Remit to:

MORTGAGE PAYMENT

STATE BANK OF OHIO
19622 High Street
Maplewood, OH 44921
(419) 555-3243

Jamal and Keisha Booker
402 Stanton Drive
Maplewood, OH 44922

Date Due: 4/5/--
Amount Due: $830.00
Amount Due After 4/5/--: $842.00
Loan Number: KJB 0987

Form 66

Capital
Service Station

DATE: 4/2
TIME: 5:21 pm
STATION #: 324

REGULAR $15.25
TOTAL DUE $15.25
DEBIT CARD PYMT $15.25
CHANGE DUE $00.00

Form 67

Thank You for Shopping
FAMILY FOODS

DATE: 4/2   TIME: 6:08

SALAD BAR   2.72
FROZEN JUICE   1.19
FROZEN JUICE   1.19

DELI   2.39
BAKERY   1.98
BANANAS
  1.55 LB @ .59/LB   .91

SUBTOTAL   65.69
TAX*   2.25
TOTAL   67.94
DEBIT PYMT   67.94

115

Form 68

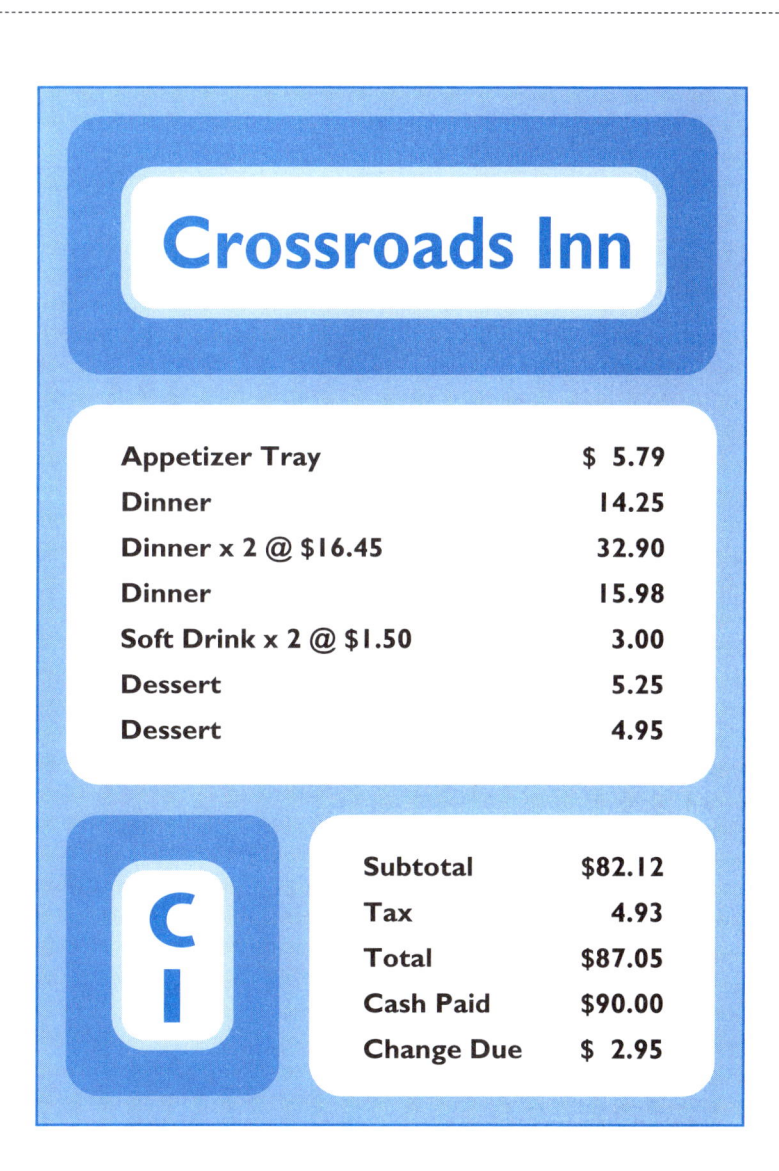

Small Treasures

Bracelet
#096 3241 $17.59

Gift Card
#005 8724 $2.49

Subtotal $20.08
Tax $1.20
Total Due $21.28

Paid by Check $21.28

Form 69

Crossroads Inn

Appetizer Tray	$ 5.79
Dinner	14.25
Dinner x 2 @ $16.45	32.90
Dinner	15.98
Soft Drink x 2 @ $1.50	3.00
Dessert	5.25
Dessert	4.95

Subtotal	$82.12
Tax	4.93
Total	$87.05
Cash Paid	$90.00
Change Due	$ 2.95

Form 1040-ES   Department of the Treasury – Internal Revenue Service

Estimated Tax Worksheet (keep for your records)

1	Adjusted gross income you expect next year (see instructions).	1
2	• If you plan to itemize deductions, enter the estimated total of your itemized deductions. **Caution:** *If line 1 above is over $139,500 ($69,750 if married filing separately), your deduction may be reduced. See Pub. 505 for details.* • If you do not plan to itemize deductions, enter your standard deduction from page 2.	2
3	Subtract line 2 from line 1	3
4	Exemptions. Multiply $3,050 by the number of personal exemptions. If you can be claimed as a dependent on another person's return, your personal exemption is not allowed. **Caution:** *See Pub. 505 to figure the amount to enter if line 1 above is over: $209,250 if married filing jointly or qualifying widow(er); $174,400 if head of household; $139,500 if single; or $104,625 if married filing separately*	4
5	Subtract line 4 from line 3	5
6	**Tax.** Figure your tax on the amount on line 5 by using the **Tax Rate Schedules** on page 2. **Caution:** *If you have a net capital gain, see Pub. 505 to figure the tax*	6
7	Alternative minimum tax from Form 6251	7
8	Add lines 6 and 7. Also include any tax from Forms 4972 and 8814 and any recapture of the education credits (see instructions above)	8
9	Credits (see instructions above). **Do not** include any income tax withholding on this line . .	9
10	Subtract line 9 from line 8. If zero or less, enter -0-	10
11	Self-employment tax (see instructions above). Estimate of net earnings from self-employment $ .... ; if **$87,000 or less,** multiply the amount by 15.3%; if **more than $87,000,** multiply the amount by 2.9%, add $10,788.00 to the result, and enter the total. **Caution:** *If you also have wages subject to social security tax, see Pub. 505 to figure the amount to enter*	11
12	Other taxes (see instructions on page 5)	12
13a	Add lines 10 through 12	13a
b	Earned income credit, additional child tax credit, and credits from **Form 4136** and **Form 8885**	13b
c	**Total estimated tax.** Subtract line 13b from line 13a. If zero or less, enter -0-	13c
14a	Multiply line 13c by 90% (66 2/3% for farmers and fishermen) . . .	14a	
b	Enter the tax shown on your previous tax return (110% of that amount if you are not a farmer or fisherman and the adjusted gross income shown on line 36 of that return is more than $150,000 or, if married filing separately, more than $75,000)	14b	
c	**Required annual payment to avoid a penalty.** Enter the **smaller** of line 14a or 14b . . .	14c
	Caution: *Generally, if you do not prepay (through income tax withholding and estimated tax payments) at least the amount on line 14c, you may owe a penalty for not paying enough estimated tax. To avoid a penalty, make sure your estimate on line 13c is as accurate as possible. Even if you pay the required annual payment, you may still owe tax when you file your return. If you prefer, you may pay the amount shown on line 13c. For details, see Pub. 505.*	
15	Income tax withheld and estimated to be withheld during 20-- (including income tax withholding on pensions, annuities, certain deferred income, etc.)	15
16	Subtract line 15 from line 14c. (**Note:** *If zero or less or line 13c minus line 15 is less than $1,000, stop here. You are not required to make estimated tax payments.*)	16
17	If the first payment you are required to make is due April 15, enter ¼ of line 16 (minus any overpayment from last year that you are applying to this installment) here, and on your payment voucher(s) if you are paying by check or money order.	17

Form 71

Sumida's
LAWN & GARDEN

MULCH $10.36
    4 @ $2.59
GARDEN HOSE $18.49
NOZZLE $12.25

SUBTOTAL $41.10
TAX .... $ 2.47
TOTAL DUE $43.57
CHECK PAID $43.57

THANK YOU

Form 72

Thank You for Shopping
FAMILY FOODS

DATE: 4/8　　　　TIME: 2:56

PORK CHOPS
  1.25 LB @ 4.25/LB　　5.31
BREAD　　　　　　　　　　2.25
MILK　　　　　　　　　　　2.49

BAGELS　　　　　　　　　1.29
CEREAL　　　　　　　　　4.25

SUBTOTAL　　　　　　　70.43
TAX*　　　　　　　　　　1.89
TOTAL　　　　　　　　　72.32
DEBIT PYMT　　　　　　72.32

Form 73

Keisha and Jamal Booker
402 Stanton Drive
Maplewood, OH 44922

Universal Cellular

Account No.: 419-555-9113

Amount Due by 4/14/--: $27.45

Universal Cellular, Inc.
Dept. 2510
South Bay, CA 94199

Save this portion for your records.

Monthly Service Charges

    Basic Package $19.95

    Call Waiting 1.50

Roaming Charges

    22 minutes @ .20 per minute 4.40

Taxes 1.60

Total Charges $27.45

Universal Cellular
Your Global Connection

Form 74

Jamal and Keisha Booker
402 Stanton Drive
Maplewood, OH 44922

Acct. No. 621-BT
Amount Due $112.28
Date Due 4/16/--

TCG&E

Tri-County Gas & Electric
P.O. Box 13579
Maplewood, OH 44920

Detach and return this portion with your payment.

BILLING EXPLANATION

BILLING PERIOD	ITEM	CURRENT CHARGES
3/1 – 3/31	Gas Meter #2216	$36.12
	Electricity Meter #55319M	$76.16

Questions? Please call 419-555-4679 for service.

TRI-COUNTY GAS & ELECTRIC

Form 75

TDS Satellite TV

Amount Due: $39.99
Due Date: 4/15/--

Account No.: 3XTS696

Keisha and Jamal Booker
402 Stanton Drive
Maplewood, OH 44922

TDS Satellite TV
2222 Newton Boulevard
Waycross, OR 97297

Keep this statement for your records.

Top Choice Basic with Local Channels $37.73

Sales Tax 2.26

    Total $39.99

For service from 3/1/-- to 4/1/--.

Account No.: 3XTS696

Upgrade to premium service NOW, and receive 5 pay-per-view movies FREE!

TDS Satellite TV

Form 76

Marta Reyes, CFP
Certified Financial Planner   (419) 555-6820

28 Lexington Ave., Suite C
Maplewood, OH 44920

Client Name	Keisha & Jamal Booker
Service Provided	Financial assessment & advice
Date	4/10/--
Amount $275.00	Paid By Check
Signature	Marta Reyes

Form 77

Capital Service Station

DATE: 4/11
TIME: 9:26 pm
STATION #: 324

REGULAR — $14.11
TOTAL DUE — $14.11
DEBIT CARD PYMT — $14.11
CHANGE DUE — $00.00

Form 78

State of Ohio

VEHICLE REGISTRATION EXPIRATION NOTICE

Amount Due: $55.00

Keisha Booker
402 Stanton Drive
Maplewood, OH 44922

Vehicle Plate No. _____ PKX 703
Plate Category _____ Passenger
Vehicle Type _____ 4S
Year _____ 2001
VIN _____ 2PSTOX5822RL08917
County _____ Franklin

YOUR VEHICLE REGISTRATION EXPIRES ON: 4/20/--

Make checks payable to the Ohio Department of Motor Vehicles.

- -

Return this portion with your check or money order.

Name: Keisha Booker
SSN: 912-65-0018

Fees: License Fee $49.00
         Service Charge $6.00
Total Amount Due: $55.00

Date Due: 4/20/--

Ohio Dept. of Motor Vehicles
P.O. Box 721
Columbus, OH 43216

Maplewood Hospital

Employee 401(k) Enrollment Form

Account Number: MH 11672 - 4 - 98 - KL

Employee Name: _____

Social Security Number: _____

Birthdate: _____

Marital Status: _____

1. What percentage of your pre-tax income do you wish to contribute? (6% maximum) _____ %

2. Indicate the percentage of your contributions you wish to contribute to these options: (10% increments; must total 100%)

    Government Money Trust _____

    Government Intermediate Fund _____

    Balanced Mutual Fund _____

    Blue Chip Fund _____

    International Fund _____

    Aggressive Growth Fund _____

3. Spouse Primary Beneficiary: _____

4. Non-spouse Primary Beneficiary

    Name 1: _____ Relationship _____

    Name 2: _____ Relationship _____

_____   _____
Employee Signature   Date

Form 80

Thank You for Shopping
FAMILY FOODS

DATE: 4/14   TIME: 5:41

COFFEE	6.49
PASTA	1.29
CHICKEN	
1.08 LB @ 4.19/LB	4.53
COOKIES	2.85
CHEESE	4.47
FLOUR	2.19
SUBTOTAL	62.46
TAX*	2.25
TOTAL	64.71
DEBIT PYMT	64.71

Form 81

From: autoconfirm@pilotnet.com
Sent: April 14, 20—
To: kjbooker@pilotnet.com
Subject: Payment Confirmation

Dear Pilot customer,

Your credit card has been charged this month's Internet connection fee.

Amount: $21.95

For: March 14–April 14, 20—

Charged to: WorldCard # ****0908

Customer:
Keisha and Jamal Booker
402 Stanton Drive
Maplewood, OH 44922
Email: kjbooker@pilotnet.com

From:
Pilot Internet Connections
665 Wellfleet Plaza
San Francisco, CA 94101

For help in using our service, please visit our online customer support at www.pilotnet.com/support. To view your account details, please log onto your account from our home page www.pilotnet.com. For billing questions, you may contact us by email at customersupport@pilotnet.com, or call 1-800-555-9000.

Thank you for choosing Pilot Internet Connections!

Form 82

Goldberg's Hardware

PAINT	2 @ 18.67	37.34
TRIM PAINT		20.86
BRUSH		9.85
ROLLER KIT		13.17
SUB		81.22
TAX		4.87
AMT OWED		86.09
AMT PAID		86.09

Form 83

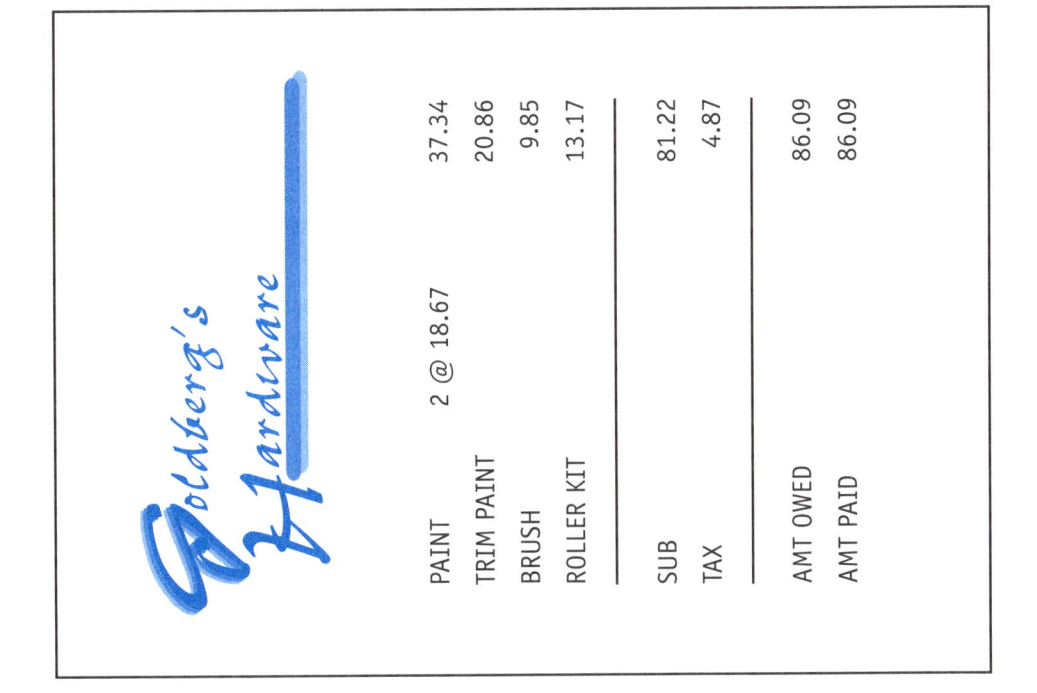

Jamal and Keisha Booker
402 Stanton Drive
Maplewood, OH 44922

PaxCo INSURANCE

Amount Due: $47.50
Date Due: 4/20/--
Account No.:   447–OHG

PaxCo Insurance Co.
280 Mesa Blvd.
Los Angeles, CA 90064

Retain this statement for your records.

Billing Period	Insurance Type	Amount
3/1 – 3/31	Standard Homeowner's Coverage	$47.50
	Total	$47.50

PaxCo INSURANCE

Due Date   4/20/--

For customer service, call (800) 555–2820.

Form 84

Donna's Uniforms

1 Scrubs Top	$13.99
1 Scrubs Pants	$15.95
Subtotal	$29.94
Tax	$1.80
Total	$31.74
Check Paid	$31.74

Form 85

Thank You for Shopping
FAMILY FOODS

DATE: 4/21   TIME: 5:23

ICE CREAM	4.27
RICE MIX	1.96
MILK	1.59
ORANGES	
3/1.50	3.00
LETTUCE	
.72 LB @ 1.74/LB	1.25
SUBTOTAL	46.72
TAX*	1.10
TOTAL	47.82
DEBIT PYMT	47.82

Form 86

Capital
Service Station

DATE: 4/21
TIME: 6:15 pm
STATION #: 324

REGULAR	$12.72
TOTAL DUE	$12.72
CASH PYMT	$13.00
CHANGE DUE	$00.28

Form 87

STATE BANK OF OHIO
AUTOMATED TELLER MACHINE

DATE: 4/24
TIME: 6:12 pm
CHECKING ACCOUNT #: 334-067214
WITHDRAWAL AMOUNT: $60.00

Form 88

La Maison
Fine French Dining

1 Dinner	$18.65
1 Side Salad	4.35
1 Dinner	19.75
2 Soft Drinks	3.00
Subtotal	$45.75
Tax	2.75
Total Due	$48.50
Cash Paid	$50.00
Change	$1.50

Form 89

🌲 **Pinetree Playhouse** 🌲
presents
The Lion King
SEAT 16D
Price: $25.00
Service Fee: $2.50   Total Price: $27.50

🌲 **Pinetree Playhouse** 🌲
presents
The Lion King
SEAT 16E
Price: $25.00
Service Fee: $2.50   Total Price: $27.50

141

Form 90

Dr. Heather Byrd, M.D.
118 Medical Center Dr.
Maplewood, OH 44919
(419) 555-5652

DATE	PATIENT NAME	SERVICE	FEE
4/25/--	Jamal Booker	Annual exam	$93.00
		TOTAL FEE	$93.00
		PATIENT COPAY.	$30.00
		INSURER'S COPAY.	$63.00

Form 91

Remit to:

CAR LOAN PAYMENT

STATE BANK OF OHIO
19622 High Street
Maplewood, OH 44921
(419) 555-3243

Jamal and Keisha Booker
402 Stanton Drive
Maplewood, OH 44922

Date Due: 4/29/--
Amount Due: $216.40
Amount Due After 4/29/--: $238.10
Loan Number: KJB 1163

Form 92

Jamal and Keisha Booker
402 Stanton Drive
Maplewood, OH 44922

Due Date 4/29/--
Amount $240.60
Car Loan I.D.# 0-14967-822

Oak Grove Bank

1502 Whitehurst Ave.
Maplewood, OH 44920

Form 93

Corner Mart

Deodorant	1.97
Shampoo	2.74
Greeting Card	2.15
Shave Gel	3.62

Sub: $10.48
Tx: $0.63
Total: $11.11
Check Pd: $11.11

Please Come Again!

City of Maplewood

Office of Property Taxes

Owners: Jamal and Keisha Booker
Property: 402 Stanton Drive
Maplewood, OH 44922

Tax Period: 11/1/-- to 4/30/--
Tax Amount: $1,650.00
Tax Due: 5/5/--

Make your check or money order payable to:

City of Maplewood

Thank you.

Return this statement with your check or money order.

Jamal and Keisha Booker
402 Stanton Drive
Maplewood, OH 44922

Property tax due: $1,650.00
Date due: 5/5/--

City of Maplewood Tax Office
One Town Square
Maplewood, OH 44920

Form 95

STATE BANK OF OHIO   HOME LOAN QUALIFYING APPLICATION

APPLICANT INFORMATION

APPLICANT
Name _____
Address _____
Home Ph _____ Work Ph _____
SSN _____ Age _____
Dependent Children _____ Ages _____
Employer _____
Address _____

CO-APPLICANT
Name _____
Address _____
Home Ph _____ Work Ph _____
SSN _____ Age _____
Dependent Children _____ Ages _____
Employer _____
Address _____

ELEGIBILITY REQUIREMENTS

☐ Y ☐ N   I am 18 years old or older and a U.S. citizen or resident alien.

☐ Y ☐ N   I have not declared bankruptcy in the last 7 years.

☐ Y ☐ N   I plan to live in the property.

☐ Y ☐ N   I have not paid any bill late in the last 2 years.

INCOME INFORMATION

	APPLICANT	CO-APPLICANT
Base Employment Income	_____	_____
Overtime	_____	_____
Commissions	_____	_____
Rental Income	_____	_____
TOTAL	_____	_____

ASSETS

Checking Account _____
Savings Account _____
Retirement Accounts _____
CDs/Money Markets _____
Other Investments _____
Non-liquid Assets _____
(cars, personal items, house)

LIABILITIES

           MONTHLY PAYMENT

Mortgage Payment _____
Credit Card Debt _____
Alimony _____
Child Care/Support _____
Other Loans _____

APPLICANT SIGNATURE & DATE _____

CO-APPLICANT SIGNATURE & DATE _____

STATE BANK OF OHIO

Keisha and Jamal Booker
402 Stanton Drive
Maplewood, OH 44922

Statement prepared on:	4/28/--
Opening Balance:	$6,922.82
Closing Balance:	$3,039.75
Account Number:	334-067214

Checks

Check No.	Date Paid	Amount
1312	4/4	830.00
1313	4/5	21.28
1314	4/9	2,770.00
1315	4/9	43.57
1316	4/13	275.00
1317	4/15	55.00

Check No.	Date Paid	Amount
1318	4/19	420.00
1319	4/18	86.09
1320	4/21	47.50
1321	4/21	31.74
1322	4/25	1,500.00
1323	4/28	30.00

Debits and Withdrawals

Date	Amount	Description
4/2	15.25	Debit transaction: Capital Service Station
4/2	67.94	Debit transaction: Family Foods
4/8	72.32	Debit transaction: Family Foods
4/9	27.45	Online payment: Universal Cellular
4/9	112.28	Online payment: Tri-County Gas & Electric
4/9	39.99	Online payment: TDS Satellite TV
4/11	14.11	Debit transaction: Capital Service Station
4/14	64.71	Debit transaction: Family Foods
4/21	47.82	Debit transaction: Family Foods
4/24	60.00	ATM Withdrawal
4/28	3.00	Service Charge: Online Bill Payment Service

Deposits

Date	Amount	Description
4/15	1,251.98	Direct Payroll Deposit: Maplewood Hospital
4/20	1,500.00	Deposit

STATE BANK OF OHIO

Account Reconciliation Form

1. Enter closing balance from statement. $ _____

2. List deposits/credits made after statement date:

DATE	AMOUNT	DATE	AMOUNT	DATE	AMOUNT

Enter total of above deposits and credits. $ _____

3. Compute subtotal (#1 plus #2). $ _____

4. List checks, withdrawals, and debits not yet paid by bank:

CHECK NO. OR DATE	AMOUNT	CHECK NO. OR DATE	AMOUNT	CHECK NO. OR DATE	AMOUNT

Enter total of above checks, withdrawals, and debits. $ _____

5. Enter revised bank balance (#3 minus #4). $ _____

6. Enter checkbook balance $ _____
   Subtract service charges $ _____
   Add interest paid $ _____
   Enter result $ _____

Final amount on Line 6 should be the same as your revised bank balance on Line 5. If not, please consult section below.

If revised bank balance is MORE than your checkbook balance:	If revised bank balance is LESS than your checkbook balance:
(a) Have you checked your addition and subtraction above and in your checkbook?	(a) Have you checked your addition and subtraction above and in your checkbook?
(b) Does the above list include all of your outstanding checks, withdrawals, and debits?	(b) Have you deducted service and other bank charges in your checkbook?
(c) Have you added all ATM deposits in your checkbook?	c) Have you deducted all ATM withdrawals in your checkbook?
(d) Have you added all credits and advances in your checkbook?	(d) Have you deducted all credit line and preauthorized payments in your checkbook?

In case of errors or questions about your account, call (800) 555-3000.

BUDGET WORKSHEET FOR _____

Monthly Income

Gross Pay .... _____
Taxes/Deductions .... _____
Net Pay .... _____

Monthly Expenses

Savings/Debt Payoff .... _____
Savings Accounts .... _____
Investments .... _____
Loan Payments .... _____
Other (_____) _____

Home .... _____
Rent/Mortgage Payment ..... _____
Property Taxes .... _____
Utilities .... _____
Phone/Pager Service .... _____
Cable/Satellite TV Service..... _____
Internet Service.................... _____
Home Maintenance.............. _____
Home/Renter's Insurance ..... _____
Home Furnishings................ _____
Home Electronics .... _____

Food/Sundries .... _____
Food .... _____
Personal Care Items .... _____
Small Home Care Items .... _____

Personal .... _____
Clothes & Shoes .... _____
Haircuts/Salon Services.......... _____
Dry Cleaning/Laundry........... _____
Gym Membership .... _____
Life Insurance .... _____

Transportation .... _____
Car Loan Payment .... _____
Car Insurance .... _____
Gasoline/Oil.......................... _____
Car Maintenance .... _____
License/Registration Fees ..... _____
Bus/Subway Fares .... _____

Entertainment................................. _____
Restaurant Meals .... _____
Event Fees/Tickets................ _____
Travel Expenses .... _____

Miscellaneous .... _____
Child Care Expenses .... _____
Gifts .... _____
Donations/Charities .... _____
Pet/Hobby Expenses .... _____
Education Fees .... _____
Bank Service Charges........... _____

Health Care .... _____
Doctor & Dental Fees .... _____
Prescription Medicines......... _____
Glasses/Contact Lenses........ _____

Column 1 Total .... _____   **Column 2 Total** .... _____

Grand Total .... _____

Form 97

153

Glossary

assets cash and anything of value that you own

automated teller machine (ATM) a bank computer that allows you to make transactions, such as deposits and withdrawals, without actually going inside the bank

automatic bill payment making ongoing bill payments by granting the company the authority to charge the amount to your credit card or deduct it from your bank account at stated intervals, such as monthly, without sending you a bill first; the transactions appear on your bank or credit card statements

average a "typical" number in a set of numbers, calculated by adding the numbers in the set and dividing the sum by the number of numbers in the set; for example, the average of 32, 33, and 34 is 32 + 33 + 34 = 99, divided by 3, which equals 33

bonds investments in corporations or governments that represent loans that these organizations must repay by a specified date

budget a plan for dividing up your income among saving and spending options

cancelled checks checks that have been processed through the banking system and the amounts have been subtracted from your checking account

certificate of deposit (CD) a deposit in a savings institution that earns a stated interest rate for a specific period of time

Certified Financial Planners investment professionals who help their clients achieve their financial goals through sound planning and investing

checkbook register a form for recording all deposits to and withdrawals from your checking account, including written checks and electronic transactions

claims requests made to an insurance company to pay the amount due under the terms of the policy

copayment under certain health care plans, such as an HMO or PPO, the portion of the total medical fee or prescription cost that the patient pays

credit an agreement to borrow money now and repay it later, usually with monthly payments

debit card bank card that you can use like a check to pay for purchases at a store or make transactions on your account using an automated teller machine

dependent for tax purposes, someone who relies on someone else for financial support

direct deposit method of payment in which funds are deposited directly into the payee's bank account; often used for paychecks and tax refunds

diversify distributing funds among a variety of investments to reduce the overall risk; for example, mutual funds diversify by pooling the funds of many individual investors to purchases the stocks and bonds of a wide variety of organizations

dividends part of a corporation's profits paid out to its stockholders

down payment the first, typically large, payment on an expensive item made at the time of purchase

estimate written document, provided before work begins, showing how much the service is likely to cost

exemptions deductions from taxable income allowed by the IRS

finance charge any fee for the use of credit; could include a monthly fee for use of a credit card, interest, and other fees

finances money and other resources

401(k) account a tax-deferred retirement savings plan offered to employees by their employer

franchise one of a chain of individually owned businesses authorized to sell the chain's products; for example, McDonald's restaurants are owned by different people but they all sell McDonald's products

fringe benefits any compensation other than wages that you receive from you employer, such as paid vacation time and paid life insurance.

gross pay total earned before taxes and other deductions have been subtracted

health maintenance organization (HMO) corporation made up of doctors and other health professionals who provide a range of health care services to employee groups for a set monthly rate

homeowner's insurance insurance that pays part of the cost of replacing stolen possessions and repairing damage to the owner's house caused by fire, storms, or other hazards

individual retirement account (IRA) tax-deferred investment account for people who do not participate in a retirement plan through their employer

installments payments made at regular intervals to pay off a large debt

interest fee for using borrowed money, usually expressed as a rate, or percentage of the unpaid balance

investing allowing others to use your extra money to conduct their business, in exchange for which you earn interest

liabilities money owed

life insurance insurance that pays a stated amount to a named person if the insured person dies

line of credit maximum amount of unpaid debt allowed on the account

money market account a savings account whose funds are invested in safe types of securities; the interest rate goes up and down a small amount as the values of the securities change

mortgage home loan

mutual fund a collection of stocks and bonds purchased by a professional fund manager with a pool of money from many investors

net pay amount of money you take home after taxes and other deductions have been removed

net worth dollar value of all the things you own, minus the sum of your debts

outstanding check a check that has not finished its processing route from the payee's bank back to yours, so your bank has not yet subtracted the amount from your account

paycheck stub an attachment to your paycheck that shows how much you earned and how much money was deducted for taxes, health insurance, etc.

payee the person or business to whom the check is written

payment voucher a form mailed with a check to identify what the check is to be used for

personal identification number (PIN) your "secret code" that allows you, and no one else, to use your account

preferred provider organization (PPO) a network of doctors and health facilities that have contracted with employers to offer health services to their employees

premium regular payment required to purchase insurance

prove cash to total and verify the transactions in your financial record

quotation a written description of the terms and price of something you wish to buy, such as an insurance policy

real estate land and any buildings on it

Glossary

reconcile a checkbook to make sure that your record of checking account transactions matches your bank's records

refinance take out a new loan to pay off an existing loan, usually to get a lower interest rate

refund for income taxes, the excess amount of money returned to you if too much tax was withheld from your paychecks during the year

renter's insurance a type of home insurance that covers personal property in a rented residence in case of loss from fire, storms, theft, or other hazards

risk (investment) chance that your investment may lose value, resulting in loss of interest or even loss of the money you invested

roll over to reinvest money in the same or similar account

Roth IRA retirement account in which you pay income taxes on your contributions but do not pay taxes when you withdraw the money at retirement; as a result, the account's earnings are tax-free

self-employed working for yourself, running your own business

service charge a fee charged by a bank for performing services for you; for example, a bank may deduct a service charge from your account for processing each check your write and for use of the automated teller machines

shares of stock units of ownership in a corporation

stockholders investors who are part-owners a corporation because they own shares of its stock

sundries small personal and home care items typically found in a grocery or drug store, such as shampoo, light bulbs, toilet paper, etc.

taxable income the total income on which you must pay tax

tax credits amounts you may subtract from the tax you owe

tax-deferred income income on which taxes are put off until a later date, such as retirement age

term life insurance life insurance policy that pays a stated amount if the insured person dies within the time period stated in the policy; unlike other kinds of life insurance, term policies have no savings component

transaction event that involves money coming in or going out

utilities essential services, such as gas and electricity, water, and garbage collection, often provided by government-regulated companies

voiding a check destroying a check by writing the word "VOID" in large letters across it to so that no one can cash it

withholding amounts that employers subtract from employees' paychecks and send to the government as payments on the employees' income taxes